THE
EMPOWERED
CHRISTIAN WOMAN:

The Promise of New Life

BY
ANITA LANTZ

xulon
PRESS

CONTENTS

This book is dedicated to my children,
Lauren and Craig, and to the memory of my son, Mark,
their brother waiting in heaven,
and to my grandsons, Craig Jr., Charles, and Joseph;
all of whom are God's gifts to me and my great joy and blessing.

May each of you allow God to teach you His Wisdom, which
is above man's wisdom, that you might achieve to your fullest
potential and rise higher than you dreamed possible,
to be an influence for good in the world.

*

*"How much better to get wisdom than gold,
and good judgment than silver!"*
(Proverbs 16:16, NLT).

ACKNOWLEDGMENTS

W riting a book has many phases and although some are arduous, all have been a labor of love for me. First and foremost, my love, respect, and appreciation go to the six exceptional women who graciously and enthusiastically accepted my invitation to be part of this book by contributing their stories, written in their own words: Joy Briggs, Cara Suchman, Joyce Marion, Elaine Keith, Ruth Foster, and Judy Ross.

I appreciate the fact that time is of a premium for most people; so in addition, my heartfelt thanks go to Cara Suchman, for her ability and time given to accurately transcribing the taped stories of two of these women; to Tressa Ferrella, for her expertise and time spent to edit my first chapter and to Sharon Keaney, for her time spent critiquing and offering valid and compelling suggestions for my second chapter, both of which were included as sample chapters in my all important *Formal Book Proposal*; and to Maureen Nebinger, for her time spent reading my entire pre-submitted *Proposal* as well as for her encouraging comments. Also, my thanks go to Ruth Foster as well as Bill and Joy Briggs, for reading the entire first draft of my manuscript and expressing their encouragement and belief in this book's benefit to all women, and their belief in its timeliness.

My special thanks go to Judy Ross, whose help throughout this project was invaluable to me. From the beginning, she believed in this book and felt led of God to give her time and energy to assist me with my self-editing, by reading aloud to me the first to the final drafts. In doing so, her encouragement and her honest responsive, penetrating insights contributed in the editing, were most important to me.

Finally, I thank my God for empowering and enabling me to write and complete this book.

INTRODUCTION

O ur back cover briefly, but intriguingly, hints at what we can expect to learn in this book about *The Empowered Christian Woman*. Again, we see that woman across the room. She looks happy, self-confident, unflappable, and we notice her easy laugh. Once more, we say to ourselves, "Now that's how I wish I felt!" She appears to be a woman without a care in the world; who successfully endeavors to "look her best, do her best, and be her best." We are sure she doesn't know what trials and hardships are. And yes, we admit that we wish we had her life. Our own feels overwhelming with daily struggles and trials; not to mention the unfulfilled expectations and the emotional pain that goes with it all. Today, we are expected to play so many different roles, making life more challenging and stressful than it has ever been. We feel powerless to overcome our life condition and the trials of life we've been dealt. We are surviving, but just barely.

Whether we are married, widowed, divorced or never married singles, we have all felt like that at some time in our lives. None of us escapes these trials of life. However, in my public ministry to women, I have observed that there is a huge difference in how we handle our trials. So, what makes one so defeated and hopeless and allows another to remain strong and optimistic?

To begin our discovery to learn that answer, this book first addresses the question: "What do women want?" Whatever is our marital status, life condition, race, ethnicity, social or economic position, circumstances, or religious persuasion, we learn we are more alike than we are different. We all want to be the best woman we can be.

It is shocking to realize that *the woman across the room* is experiencing some of the same type trials we are going through, but it's true. The difference for her is that she has chosen "God's answer," *the promise of new life,* which enables her to live as an *empowered* woman. That is the reason '*she appears to be a woman without a care in the world.*' She has learned that she can live a stress-free and peaceful life—enabling her to reflect that image we admire, of a *happy, confident, and unflappable* woman, who has *an easy laugh.*

I'm sure you agree that at no time has there been a greater need than now, for women everywhere to discover they, too, can thrive in their trials—no matter what is happening in this chaotic, unstable world, nation, and culture—or in their personal lives.

If you are a woman from eighteen into your senior years, this book is written for you. Together we will explore the Bible truth presented and the evidence of that truth revealed in its featured stories of biblical characters and contemporary women.

Whether you are Christian or non-Christian, I know you are a God-seeking woman like me and the six other women you will meet in the upcoming chapters or you would not have chosen to read this book. My hope is that you will keep an open mind and open heart while doing so. It offers the opportunity for you to see where you are spiritually, according to Scripture, and to determine where you want to be.

I suggest that you will gain the greatest benefit from everything shared here if you will set aside, for now, all of your preconceived notions about whether or not you believe God does, in fact, hold the answer to your being able to live an *empowered* life. If you decide He does, the choice to embrace that life will be entirely up to you.

After reading this book, if you decide that *the promise of new life* is *not* the *answer* you've been looking for; then all you've lost is the few hours it took to read it. But, if it turns out to, indeed, be your *answer,* as it has been for me, the six women whose stories you will have read, and countless others over the past 2000 plus years; then you have gained a *new life* in Christ, with all of its benefits—a life so much better and more rewarding than you could have otherwise imagined possible.

You will no longer be powerless to deal with your challenges and trials. Instead of "barely surviving," you will find yourself "thriving" in the midst of them. You, too, will be living a stress-free and peaceful life that enables you to always "look your best, do your best, and be your best"— whatever your age—reflecting the image of an *empowered Christian woman*, like *the woman across the room*.

I, as well as each woman who contributed her story, pray that this book will speak hope and encouragement to you and women throughout the world, living in today's precarious and challenging times.

Chapter One

GETTING ACQUAINTED: WOMAN-TO-WOMAN, HEART-TO-HEART

L ife is challenging for women on so many levels. Today, a magnitude of pressures and challenges that threaten the security of our country and our families are being felt on a deeply personal level. We are all dealing with one problem or another; suffering in some way to one degree or another.

Throughout the history of the world, individual nations and mankind in general have always had personal struggles. However, today, not only our nation and society but also the entire world seems to be having a breakdown right before our eyes. Many people are greatly distressed when watching scenes of national and international disturbances being played out on the news day and night: wars, terrorism, catastrophic natural and man-made disasters, extreme weather conditions, famine, political unrest, economic failures, skyrocketing government debt, increased taxes, outrageous immorality and atrocious violent crimes. Who would ever have believed the media would have so many family-related crimes to report about spouses killing spouses, parents killing children, and children killing parents and grandparents?

Actually, all of this appears to be threatening our western culture and way of life, as we have known it. It seems that some people in our society as well as others throughout the world have lost their moral compass. Globally, greed and corruption abound and the moral line between right and wrong is no longer clearly defined but rather, it is abhorrently blurred. It appears that everything *evil* is called "good" and everything *good* is called "evil." (See Isaiah 5:20.) Some notable politicians, celebrities, and other public figures whose notorious acts or moral indiscretions have been exposed, have had little or no public outrage to bear and generally have been given a pass, so to speak, to go right on enjoying their same popularity. It seems as though an excess of tolerance has made our society insensitive to the need for accountability. It is easy for those of us who adhere to a higher moral standard to feel estranged from our own culture. Not only our nation but also the whole world is fraught with instability, injustice, violence, and moral decline, resulting in an alarming rate of personal sufferings. Many dread what might happen next.

There are legitimate reasons why women, and even men, fear for our nation, and for our families. With that kind of fear can often come the stresses of constant worry, nervous tension, anxiety and depression. Many people go to great lengths to fight these debilitating symptoms. However, no one can escape what is happening in the world, our nation, or our culture. The reality is that no one can adequately have total freedom from the effects of it all touching our personal lives or the lives of our loved ones.

We shouldn't be surprised by that, as none of us—Christian or not—is exempt from experiencing trials in this life. Jesus tells us in His Word that, "Here on earth you will have many trials and sorrows. But take heart, because I have overcome the world" (John 16:33b, NLT).

I began to think more about the trials women, in particular, face. Considering the uncertain times in which we live, many of us find ourselves not only worried about the direction our nation's economy and society are going but also, the direction our personal lives and the lives of our loved ones are going—making our futures decidedly unsure. When it comes to the trials of life, we all have heard the universal cliché: "That which does not kill us, only makes us stronger." But I don't think most of us women are as sure of that as we once were.

Many of us feel more powerless and more vulnerable than ever before. If not in the past or if not currently, at some point all of us will individually face trials and tough challenges we have never faced before. Life happens—our health or the health of our loved ones suffer; jobs come and go; careers end; disasters occur; homes are lost; loved ones die, hearts break; love waxes and wanes, marriages end, and dreams are shattered. Life can change in an instant.

Yes, unfortunately, *life happens* and each of us must endure the trials that come our way. However, when we factor in the tumultuous times threatening our sense of security and well being, some of us might be wondering, "How can I stand strong in the face of these threatening world and national crises?" Even some Christians might be wondering, "How will I be able to stand if things get even worse?"

There is no doubt in my mind that this is the very reason for *why* I wrote this book. It was written to give you viable hope and to encourage you to believe you not only *can* successfully cope with every trial in your personal life but also, you can stand strong, without fear, no matter what is happening in the world, in the nation, or in society. And I will show you how.

Before we start our journey together, there are a few personal details I'd like to share with you in *getting acquainted*. I was born into a staunch Roman Catholic, middle-class family, and had a secure but rather uneventful childhood. In the early years of my marriage, I experienced my share of trials—unpredictable and rather bizarre trials—which you will read about in a later chapter. I would never again want to go through any one of those ordeals. But it was those severe trials, which pressed me *heart* and *soul* into crying out my desperate plea, "God... *if* you're *really* here now... please help me!" He was, and He did.

It wasn't until I received *the promise of new life* and experienced the amazing power of God, that I realized He had mercifully intervened in my trials during those early years. He had been working behind the scenes when I was yet, unaware, to change expected negative outcomes into positive ones, helping me to "survive" them. Then, after the Bible became paramount to my daily living and I gained knowledge about Jesus and learned to trust what He says in

His Word, He helped me to "thrive" in the midst of my trials. From that time forward, my family and I experienced God's healing power in miraculous ways.

As time went by, a pastor of a local Christian church heard about my testimony and invited me to share it with his congregation. To say I was shocked would be an understatement. I was certain that I could not speak before a congregation of people.

When I mentioned the invitation to my husband, he encouraged me to accept. Even so, I struggled against it, believing I was neither worthy to serve God nor did I possess the ability to speak publicly about God in this way. Nonetheless, this invitation kept me on my knees. After much prayer and specifically studying over and over again the words of Jesus Himself in the Gospels; it was made clear to me that He not only intended all of His followers to be witnesses for Him but also, He promised we would be *empowered* by the Holy Spirit to serve Him. With that, peace came to my heart and compelled me to accept the pastor's invitation; albeit, not without fear and trembling. I put all my trust in the power of God the Holy Spirit to use my words to honor Jesus. And He did.

I did not know what to expect next, but for now, I knew in my heart that invitation had been God-ordained. Soon, invitations came in from other Christian sources—both Catholic and Protestant—and also a Messianic Jewish gathering. My husband continued to encourage me to share my experience with Jesus Christ publicly.

It was God alone, who opened doors for me to speak about His *promise of new life* in Christ and its benefits. Therefore, I had the opportunity to talk and pray with a cross-section of people in places of learning, fellowship, and worship—from churches and upscale hotel banquet rooms to radio broadcast studios to both Catholic and Protestant groups gathered in the living rooms of homes.

After being a guest on the national CBS TV program, "I Believe in Miracles," I received more invitations to share my story—even with a gathering of Catholic priests and nuns. For the next nearly four decades, God opened doors for me to share my personal story and God's Bible truths with multitudes of people over Christian radio and in public venues such as, the Aglow Fellowship International chapters, the Catholic Woman's Day Conference on the Holy Spirit, and the Business and Professional Women's Clubs—to name a few.

It has always been—and ever will be—a humbling experience for me to be a witness for Christ and His love before an audience or one-on-one. I remember the especially humbling experience of being invited to be the keynote speaker for *The World Day of Prayer* observance in Columbus at which the hierarchy and laypersons of different Catholic Parishes and various Protestant Denominations joined In attendance. This observance was also taking place on the same day in other major cities in the U. S. and countries throughout the world. It was an honor and blessing I will never forget.

When my children were grown and our youngest entered college, I entered a new season of my life. In addition to speaking invitations, my husband also encouraged me to accept a nomination to serve as a trustee on the Board of Directors of a major broadcasting corporation, *The Christian Voice of Central Ohio,* which governed its three radio stations operating 24-hour programming: Two in Ohio and one in Sao Paulo, Brazil. I served as a trustee for the next seven years.

Now, before you determine that I have probably lived a charmed life since my encounter with Christ and, therefore, might not know anything about the kind of severe problems you could be going through—you should know something more about me. Along with the many spiritual and personal blessings I have experienced over the years as a follower of Christ; also, I have experienced many hard trials. Again, none of us should be surprised by that fact. As mentioned before, Jesus told His followers that 'Here on earth you will have many trials and sorrows'.

Since Jesus rescued me, I have been completely dependent on God in all of my trials and He has taken me through each one. Even after twenty-six years of being a stay-at-home wife, mother, and homemaker, working seven of those years in our home office as business partner with my husband who was a Christian for twelve years—I endured the heart-wrenching pain of his turning away from his Christian life and turning away from me, by his betrayal with a much younger woman. With the crushing pain of shattered dreams, I was forced to enter an altogether new and different season of my life—alone—except for my faithful Heavenly Father.

I continued trusting God as I re-entered the outside work force. During my "single again" years, I enjoyed several different but equally satisfying work opportunities, and God continued opening doors for me to serve Him. At the end of that period, when I retired from the local ABC Television Network affiliate after seven years, I felt impressed to decline all speaking invitations. I didn't know why. Soon, I would learn that answer.

I entered a season unlike any other. It was a hard season of loss, deep sorrow and grief. It began with the unexpected death of my only brother. Then, the following year, I faced a mother's worst nightmare, when I suffered the untimely loss of my oldest son. There is no way to describe the excruciating pain I experienced. So deep was my pain that I didn't think I could go on—except for my loving Jesus, who faithfully carried me through.

Then, the time came when I chose to move both of my parents into my home to care for them for the next several years, until they passed three years apart—the only time they had been separated in 78 years of marriage. Their individual deaths were also great losses to me, even though I knew one day I would be reunited with them as well as my son and my brother, in Heaven.

God has shown His love and faithfulness to me in all of these physical and emotional trials throughout the various seasons of my life. Actually, it was in the midst of my trials that I learned my most valuable spiritual and personal growth lessons as well as experiencing the Lord's biblical promise: "And we know that all things work together for good to them that love God... " (Rom. 8:28).

I am thoroughly convinced that without having received and fully committed myself to *the promise of new life* in Jesus Christ, I would not have known the *empowered* life that I have enjoyed all of these years. And therefore, I would not have walked in God's best plan for me. I am certain my life would neither have been filled with the spiritual and personal adventures and extraordinary life experiences I've known nor would I have enjoyed the favor of God, which continues to bless my daily living.

Without reservation, I can say that my seasons of blessings *and* my seasons of trials have both enriched my life. I learned that God would *never leave me nor forsake me;* that His presence would be with me in every trial; that in my weakness His strength would allow me to thrive in the midst of each trial; and, He would cause me to come through even stronger. Therefore, *all* of the seasons of my life could only be measured as valuable seasons of growth and maturing.

You might find yourself in one or more trials even now. It is important for you to know that I could not have spoken this Bible truth publicly for thirty-plus years and I could not have written this Bible truth you are now reading about *the promise of new life*, with all of its benefits, if I had not already experienced its proven reality in my own life. Also, it is important for you to know that there is nothing special about me because I have written Bible truth for you to read. I have not written this book because I know everything there is to know about God. But what I do know and have experienced has changed my life. I believe this same Bible truth written here can change your life, too, in a very positive way.

Together, we will look at the issues of life all of us women are faced with today and how resilient we are in the various ways we live and handle our challenges and trials. We will be confronted by the provocative question: "What do women want?" In the process of discovering the answer to that question, we also will discover together that what we women want *can* be ours.

This book's message assures each one of us that God knows exactly where we are; that He sees and hears our heart; that He values us and loves us just as we are; and that He does, indeed, have the *answer* for what we want—and need—to live the *empowered* life. I am also convinced that as we move through these chapters, we will recognize that we all have room to learn and grow in our spiritual life. I am excited by the prospect that we will be learning and growing together.

Wherever you are spiritually, I think you'll agree that at no time was there a greater need than now for women everywhere to discover that they can be *empowered* to *thrive* in their everyday personal lives. Before we get started, there is something else you should know about this book in discovering how you can live the *empowered* life.

You need to know that this book is fully Bible-based. I believe the Bible to be the divinely inspired, inerrant Word of God. I do not claim to understand every word at any given time, because I still get additional revelation as I study it and grow in my Christian life. The Bible says of itself: "All Scripture is given by inspiration of God and is profitable for doctrine, for reproof, for correction, for instruction in righteousness, that the man *(or woman)* of God may be complete, thoroughly equipped for every good work" (II Timothy 3:16-17, NKJV, Italics added).

Without that as a base, I am not sure how anyone establishes any kind of truth. For me, the Bible is absolute truth. Let me tell you more about why I believe that. I have learned that the Bible is miraculous in its giving of truth without contradiction, because although it had 40 writers, it had only one Author—God. What's more, the writers were of several different generations, living on three different continents, and their books were hand-scripted in three different languages of Hebrew, Greek, and Aramaic—so they could not have collaborated in their writings.

Think about it. In those days, people were unable to communicate with one another from a distance, except by hand-carried letters. They did not have any of the advantages we have in our highly technical age of computers, Internet, I-Pads and I-Phones. They could not telephone, send a text message, or jot off an email; and yet, their writings, inspired by God, are miraculously alike. The 66 books were written over a period of 1500 years; and all share a common theme of God's universal love for all of humanity and a common message that salvation is available to all people of all nations through the One True God. The Old Testament Scriptures foretell with amazing accuracy, the coming of the Messiah, Jesus Christ, as Savior, 2000 years before the printed New Testament introduced Him to the world.

Because I have learned that understanding and believing the Scriptures takes a revelation from God and is not just an intellectual decision, I never argue about the Bible with anyone. I do discern almost instantly whether or not they believe the Bible, but it's God's job to persuade them of what is true. I can only state the facts that I know. I have been born again of the Spirit long enough to have many truths of the Bible proven in my life, and I have witnessed the conversions of hundreds of people for whom it has also proven true.

I am reminded of a part of my friend Judy's story, which you will read in its entirety in an upcoming chapter. Having been un-churched her entire life before becoming born-again, Judy shared that even though she had never read the Bible, she had a strong opinion about it: "Who could possibly believe the Bible is actually God's Words to us? After all, it is thousands of years old and has been translated by different people into different languages. How could it be relevant for today?" But, after she experienced being born again, she felt compelled to read the Bible for herself. She opened the first book in the New Testament, the Gospel of Matthew, and began reading from verse one. When she finished the last chapter, to her own shock and amazement, she exclaimed, "It is absolutely true. I believe every word."

There are many people like Judy who reject the relevancy of the Bible before they have even read it. On the other hand, I know people who declare they are Christian and have read the Bible, but still do not believe its relevancy for today. I have heard them state their reasons: that because the Scriptures were written by men in different timeframes, written to and about different people of different cultures, they do not apply today. They also say there have been many more scrolls found over the centuries, which have not been included in the Bible, and it has been men who have chosen which of the written scrolls would be translated and included in the printed Bible. Consequently, they conclude that because man is fallible the Bible is also fallible, and cannot be trusted to be considered the Holy, inerrant, Word of God.

Their arguments never bother me and I respect what they say. Everyone is entitled to his or her opinion. However, I know while parts of what they say are true, they leave out one important component, which must be considered; and that is God, Himself. God has always worked through believers. The men who wrote the Scriptures, the men who translated the Scriptures, and the men who chose which Scriptures would make up the books of the Bible to print, were believers. How hard is it to conclude that God worked through them and divinely inspired them to do His bidding; that they were inspired by God to do what they did to give people the laws, principles, and guidelines He wanted them to have to conduct their personal lives?

While the times and cultures have changed, people have not changed, God has not changed, and God's laws and principles have not changed. Various translations of the Protestant, Greek, and Catholic Bibles do a good job of bringing some verses up to date; but even modern language retains God's originally intended message. Today, individuals—atheists and people in most religions of the world, including believers in God—follow the laws of their nation, state, and city, not realizing that they are following the laws God inspired man to write down centuries ago and are identified in the Bible. Some critics would say that the written words in the Bible are only ink on paper. But for those of us who do believe and by faith trust that God says what He means and means what He says in the Bible, He causes His Word to be supernaturally alive and functioning. For us, the Bible is a continual source of wisdom and guidance that is as relevant today as it has been to all believers down through the ages.

I have learned in my thirty-plus years in public ministry how believers and non-believers think about the Bible. I've learned that even many who claim to believe in God, actually *do not* believe what He says in the Bible. And, if we *do not* believe what the Bible says, it *will not* work for us. We *will not* have what the Bible says. For example, if we *do not* believe in repentance for which the Bible promises forgiveness of sin through Jesus; we *will not* experience the joy of knowing we are forgiven; and if we *do not* believe in healing, we *will not* experience the overwhelming gratitude of being healed. On the other hand, I have learned from personal experience, that if *we do* believe in God and *we do* believe His promises in the Bible, it works for us—but always according to God's Will and in His time. For those of us who believe the Bible, God does for us what He promises He will do. By faith, we have what the Bible says.

We all must decide for ourselves what we believe about the Bible. But, if you are among those not acquainted with the Scriptures, hopefully, you *will* give the Bible a fair trial before you decide, and ask God to show you what is true. If you have read the Bible but do not feel you understand it, let me assure you that God will open your understanding of His Word, once you have been born again of the Spirit according to Scripture. As you study the Bible, the Holy Spirit will continue to reveal truth as He draws you closer and closer.

How I feel about the Bible is based upon my personal experience. Before I was born again, I was totally ignorant of what the Bible says and everything about its origin. But after I was born again of the Spirit, my understanding was opened to believe the Bible, which renewed my mind, transformed my life, and blessed me with many of the promises of God.

Finally, since this book is biblically grounded, you will be reading about the miraculous ways in which God used His Word in the every day lives of some believers. I am convinced that at its conclusion, you will be able to make a much more informed decision as to whether or not you believe the Bible to be true.

By now, I hope you feel like we are acquainted, if only in a small way. I trust you will stay with me on what I believe will be an inspiring and informative spiritual journey through the upcoming chapters. We begin by focusing on each word in this book's title: *The Empowered Christian Woman,* which is broken down into three components: *The Woman Factor, The Christian Factor,* and *The Empowered Factor.* We will explore each part, step-by-step, revealing all of its benefits.

The chapters to follow will present the evidence of these three *factors* revealed in the stories of biblical characters as well as the testimonies of contemporary women, including my own. By the time we are finished sharing *woman-to-woman, heart-to-heart,* you will know beyond a shadow of doubt, the unconditional love Jesus Christ has for you. In addition, you will know it is His desire for you to receive *the promise of new life* to become a born again, *empowered Christian woman*—to live a contented, balanced, abundant, secure life that thrives even in the midst of trials and no matter what is happening in the world, the nation, and the culture. The choice will be left to you.

Chapter Two

THE WOMAN FACTOR: WHAT DO WOMEN WANT?

We begin this spiritual journey by answering a question that some of you might be asking yourself, "What does it mean to be an *empowered Christian woman?*" The book title has three components, which will unfold the answer as we explore them in detail. They are listed here in just the opposite order as they appear in the title.

1. Woman. Although this book's Bible truth equally applies to men—I am writing to women. We all know what it means to be a woman so that requires no definition. What we do want to discover is "What do women want?"

2. Christian. This means clearly and surely knowing we made our own decision to become a Christian: We recognized that we are sinners, and we believed with our heart and placed our faith in Jesus Christ alone and the sacrifice of His shed blood on the cross for the forgiveness of our sins, to receive salvation and the assurance of eternal life. This is the scriptural definition of being "born again of the Spirit" (whether or not we know to call it that) and its how we become a member of the family of God. You will note that the terms "the promise of new life" and "born again" are used interchangeably throughout the text.

3. Empowered. The dictionary states: "Empower: 1.) To give official authority or legal power to; and 2.) to enable." When we are *born again,* Jesus sends us God the Holy Spirit to be our *Comforter, Teacher, Helper,* and *Counselor* to guide us into all truth; He empowers us with spiritual authority to pray in the Name of Jesus; He equips us to be witnesses for Christ to others; and He enables us to reach our full potential to not only serve Jesus, but also, to enjoy a contented, happy, satisfying relationship with the Living God—all of which we will learn more about as we continue.

According to these definitions, can you consider yourself an *empowered Christian woman?* If you have any doubt about it, I encourage you to stay with me and keep reading, so you can be absolutely sure. Together, we will explore Bible truth and evidence of that truth, which will help each of us to examine where we are spiritually on this question and to consider where we want to be. Ready?

The Woman Factor

Not to be facetious but it's pretty simple to know whether or not you fit into the "woman" category. But, the question, "What do women want?" is not nearly as simple.

After thirty years of research into the "feminine soul," Sigmund Freud was unable to answer the great question: What do women want? (Source: *Life and Work* by Ernest Jones, 1953.) Many, if not most of us, who consider his question, no doubt, think it refers to only the romantic aspect of a woman's life. However, I am grateful to have discovered that Sigmund Freud's question held deep spiritual significance for the women of his day as well as the women of today. No area of our lives as women is beyond the need for an answer to that question. Although Freud failed to discover the answer in his lifetime, God has always known the answer to *what women want—* and what they need.

We know from Scripture that God wants every woman to feel valued, loved, accepted, appreciated, wanted and needed; and to know her life has a meaningful, satisfying purpose. Also, she needs to feel secure and to live a contented life. God knows that is what each woman wants, because it is what He wants for her, too. We will discover together that all of a woman's wants and needs can be met by choosing "God's answer," which is found in the transformational decision to receive by faith *the promise of new life* in His Son, Jesus Christ, to be born again of the Spirit and *empowered.*

I have experienced *God's answer;* and also, I have seen it validated many times over in my public ministry, as women had no problem recognizing it was what they had always wanted — and needed — as soon as they experienced it for themselves.

With that, I find myself recalling the thought that came to me when I felt impressed to write this book; that is, my reader-audience would be "God-seeking women, eager to learn." Considering all of you, my eighteen to senior readers, I realize that while our age, race, and martial status differ and we come from different backgrounds, religious persuasions, dissimilar life conditions and circumstances, and are dealing with diverse challenges and trials — we are more alike than different when it comes to what we want and what will fulfill our basic womanly needs. It is true. If we are *'God-seeking'* and *'eager to learn',* this book's message can change our lives.

In my public ministry, over and over, I have heard the heart-breaking stories of women both inside and outside the Church: Some were dealing with personal or extreme marriage and family problems, and believed they could no longer cope; others were unhappy and dissatisfied with the way their lives had turned out; and still many simply felt their lives were empty and without purpose. Most of them were church-going believers, who were too embarrassed to expose their problems to their priests or pastors or even Christian friends, too ashamed to ask for any kind of help at all. As a lifelong church-goer and having lived in extreme circumstances before Christ rescued me, I knew and understood their pain and shame. With absolute confidence, I assured these women that the re-creative power of God's redemptive touch could reach His children anywhere — whether they were living, humanly speaking, in the most ideal or the most extreme conditions imaginable. I am living proof of that Bible truth.

I can still recall particular women with whom I personally prayed, counseled and shared this Bible truth. Each one was taking care of her everyday life responsibilities to the best of her ability and, at the same time, many were also trying to cope with some kind of major problem—a problem not unlike those that millions of women today are experiencing—maybe even you are experiencing in your own life.

Many of those women were wives in challenging or flat-out unhappy marriages for myriad reasons. I met women who were living in disappointing, dissatisfying, or markedly dysfunctional marriages and families. Some women were living in more serious circumstances with an addicted alcoholic husband and the entire family was suffering the results of his choices and bearing his shame and humiliation. Some were suffering the same humiliation because of their husband's addiction to gambling. Other women were enduring serious personal or family medical problems—some were suffering through a personal life-threatening disease or that of a loved one, and others were experiencing depression, anxiety, or their own addiction of some kind. I met with tired women who were living with the pressures of caring for their "special needs" child; and others were juggling their time to be caregivers to elderly parents while managing their own families, homes, and some even working outside jobs.

As social ills in our nation increased during the late-80s and throughout the 90s, traditional families were being negatively affected by even more severe problems: I was ministering to mothers who were frustrated with the discipline problems of their young children, the drug and alcohol problems of their teenagers, or disappointment with the chosen path and lifestyle their young adult or grown children had taken. There were women who were still suffering the emotional wounds of a past criminal street rape, date rape, or even a devastating childhood sexual molestation by a trusted family member or other person. Some were emotionally distressed because of their husband's addiction to pornography or suffering rejection because of their husband's past or present adultery. Several women were seeking forgiveness for their own sin of adultery. Still other women were victims of spousal abuse and desperately wanting to change their extreme circumstances or looking for a way out of them.

In addition, I met with divorcees who had endured every emotional suffering you can imagine, and were in need of both emotional and spiritual healing. Several were lonely and felt desperate to find a love partner to meet their emotional and sexual needs. Some had remarried and found their blended families were not like the happy

Brady Bunch as they had expected. Others felt trapped in a second marriage that turned out to be as bad as their first, and they were now embarrassed, full of guilt for the choice they had made—and hopeless about their future. And there also were divorcees who were content in their new state of being single-again and alone, but not spiritually content. Still other divorcees were overburdened with the struggle to financially support themselves and their children and to maintain a semblance of family as a single parent and, therefore, seeking God's help to make a better life.

On the other hand, many married, widowed, divorced, remarried, and single women I met did not speak of having any type of major problem and they were basically happy but still not content. I remember a never-married single woman, who had made a successful life for herself, having chosen a career over marriage—but when she came to me, she was acutely aware of feeling an emptiness, despite her successful life. I vividly recall other women who had been actually living in ideal conditions, enjoying a lovely lifestyle and having been happy most of their lives. But at the time they came to me, they were empty nesters or widows and although they were socially active and involved in their communities, they confessed that life had lost its luster. They felt depressed and believed their lives no longer held satisfying purpose. And they recognized that they were not fully content and felt something was missing in their lives—something they could not identify. Also, there was one happily married woman, who had attended church all of her life, taught Sunday school, and was serving on the Board of her mainline denominational church when we met. On a conscious level, she thought her spiritual life was as good as it gets; yet, she still felt something was missing.

Whether consciously or unconsciously, for years some women had been constantly looking for something, anything to fill whatever was missing and the emptiness it left. They desperately needed to feel good about themselves and to believe their life counted for something. What they chose to fill that void with was productive for some and destructive for others. I have learned that no matter how ideal or financially comfortable a woman's life is—if she will receive *the promise of new life* in Christ, she *will* live in a state of true contentment and satisfying purpose.

These are a sprinkling of the general life conditions and circumstances these women I ministered to were living. The good news is that all of them responded positively to the Bible truth I shared with them and as a result, they each came to the exact same decision to choose *God's answer, the promise of new life,* to become a born again, *empowered Christian woman.*

I have not followed all of their lives, but a long-term relationship with many of them did develop. Interestingly enough, although all of these women were, indeed, from different backgrounds and religious persuasions, what had been missing in their lives had been filled with what they never knew they always wanted—*God's answer.*

Since then, I have had the privilege to witness some of the miraculous changes God made in their personal lives and in their families. They went on to experience more of God's promises, and to grow and mature spiritually in God's Word. To this day, they are still growing and still trusting the Lord to orchestrate their daily lives to fulfill His purpose. I am certain that God wants to do the same for all *God-seeking women.*

Continuing ministry opportunities in various public venues, including Christian radio broadcasts such as the one in Austin, Texas, that garnered a very large listener response, have convinced me that there is a growing number of church-going women out there who are discouraged. They have unmet expectations and personal, marriage or family problems—some extreme—with which they feel powerless to deal and overcome. Although they are women of faith and *surviving*, they are not *thriving* in their Christian life and, therefore, are looking for the answer to how they can live more victoriously.

According to the most recent U. S. Census, there are 155 million women in America today. I believe the majority of both Christian and non-Christian women are dealing with serious trials and challenges. We cannot forget that social ills have increased even more during this New Millennium. Because of that fact, women today are facing additional challenges such as a declining economy and a morally declining and dangerous society in which to raise children. The traditional family values once held dear in our society by the majority of people seem to be all but forgotten by many as a way of life. In today's cultural environment, if media news and entertainment are a true reflection of a broad-spectrum of society, then it looks like there is not only a lack of simple manners but also, a growing lack of civility. Mix "political correctness" into the equation and it fosters confusion for many of us in regard to how we should interact with one another.

Watching some of today's movies, television sitcoms and "reality shows" can negatively influence many of us women. *Reality shows,* featuring ordinary people like us who are living their lives *out loud* in front of a camera give us a *window on the world,* when it comes to modern human behaviors. Some *reality shows* shock many of us, in that women participants display unrestrained and even shameless salacious conduct, crass expressions and inappropriate language, showing a lack of self-respect. Then there are show participants who display rebellious, unruly and, sometimes, seditious conduct with one another—showing a lack of respect for others. We no longer know if art is imitating life or life is imitating art.

With all of those influences in our society today, some of us also can be greatly affected by advertising. There has always been advertising underwriting every facet of the media; but today, we are bombarded with advertising words and images on Network and Cable TV, on the Internet, and in magazines and other forms of printed materials—all of which come out of the minds of marketing geniuses. Their ideas show and tell us the kind of "idyllic" lifestyle we should enjoy to be happy. These manipulative marketing ploys reveal what our lives should look like: the house we should live in, the car we should drive, the products we should buy, the latest fashion trends we should wear, and, the vacations we should take to broaden our horizons. These marketing strategies will even show and tell us what cosmetics we should use or what drastic steps we should take to hold back "Father Time" or at least keep our faces and bodies from showing the world we are aging. I've heard it said: "We ladies should be grateful that, at least, wrinkles don't hurt." Even our adolescent and teenage children are influenced by advertising and media entertainment to the extent that although they have no idea who they are as yet, they copy the speech, behaviors, and fashion styles of rock stars and other music, TV, and movie celebrities.

Advertisers tell us we deserve to have *it all* now and do *it all* now, whether or not our bank account can sustain *it all*. The trouble is, having *it all* and doing *it all* will sometimes offer little more than pseudo happiness and throw us into debt. One of those so-called *idyllic* lifestyles can put us in a position of struggling financially to pay for the privilege. Life gets harder for any of us when we are in debt. No matter what our socio-economic level, it is a known fact that financial demands are emotionally and physically stressful and take a toll on our health, our marriage, and our family life. Nevertheless, this advertiser-driven, immediate self-gratification society in which we live today, can make it easy for women to get caught up in its cultural traps.

Another negative situation that many of us women, especially wives and mothers, fall into, is believing we have to do it all. Our self-imposed expectations demand that we care for our spouse, children and home; hold down a full or part-time job; serve our community; make time for church, school, and social activities; entertain and make perfect holiday feasts; taxi our children to any number of activities and events; and remarkably, every few years, carry a baby for nine months and give birth. We take on a hectic, fast-paced routine and become overburdened, stressed, and pressured as we try to accomplish everything on our daily priority "To Do List," to make life nicer and easier for everyone else in our family. At the end of the day, our energy tank is registering on "empty" and we are running on "fumes." Still no matter how nice we have made the day for our family, life for us always gets down to the *nitty-gritty:* our toddler is having a temper tantrum at bedtime, our teenagers are out-of-control, and our husband needs our attention—all the while we are staring at a mountain of laundry still on today's priority list. Doing it all is exhausting.

Today I find that whatever is a woman's lifestyle and circumstances, for the most part, it is a given that typically she has a demanding schedule and is handling more than one of the major life responsibilities. It constantly amazes me that most of us women actually do manage it all—and keep doing it day after day, year after year. Unfortunately, in the process, we make little or no downtime for our own basic personal needs.

At this time in America, I can appreciate the enormous responsibilities commonly shared by mothers who are rearing their children alone. My heart goes out to those of you who are military wives as well as you who are widowed or divorced, trying to be both mother and father to your children because your husband is deployed, has passed away, or is a "Deadbeat Dad" who has opted out of not only his financial support but also, his kids' lives.

Some of you, who are the primary breadwinners, are trying to increase your earning power by also juggling the hard work of college studies along with a fulltime job to elevate your life style and give your children better opportunities for the future—while at the same time, caring for all their current daily needs. And like me, many of you are caring for your *special needs* child or your parents, which can be physically and emotionally exhausting. Some of you are even raising grandchildren in mid-life. I can only imagine how challenging and physically draining that must be.

Along with everything else, like every other generation of women, many of us are experiencing the hormonal roller coaster—a crazy ride that is no fun but in fact, a real nuisance and not without its emotional and physical discomforts. Although it is all perfectly normal to go through, it sure does get in the way of doing everything we are responsible to accomplish. And ready or not, we are expected to do our share of "sparkling" at various social events, even when our hormones are all over the map.

For some, that season is already behind us and our lives are comparatively quiet and easy. But that does not necessarily mean we are off the hook. We have a whole different set of new, but typical problems to deal with, some of which come naturally with aging, like that inescapable "change." Reaching that *milestone* can have its ups and downs, and serious problems for some, but we try to keep a positive attitude and sense of humor, knowing that "this too shall pass."

And we cannot forget those who are widows, facing their lives alone after a long-term marriage. For some, it is a frightening prospect to rise above their state of deep grief and depression to go on living. But with God, we can. I know, because I watched my sister. We all know women, whether young or old, who went on to live their single-again life, with purpose.

Then, reaching the official age to carry the label of "senior citizen" is another *milestone*. With an earned retirement at this juncture, or right around the corner, life can get exciting. We can look forward to free time to *tinker* or travel as well as having time for rest and relaxation. But on the other hand, being a retired senior does have its downside. We cannot deny that many are affected by this declining economy and the loss of income, leaving us to live on only our monthly Social Security checks. We also have to consider that becoming seniors means having to deal with the onset of some sort of medical condition. Those of us who have not yet reached that point, are probably dealing with the fear of losing our health or losing our mobility or losing our car keys—because the latter means losing our independence.

We have to admit that there is an endless combination of life conditions and natural challenges for women today, no matter what their age; all very easy to identify and discuss but, sometimes, difficult to live through. However, that doesn't mean we can no longer be productive and fulfill our purpose. It might be assumed by some of the younger generation that seniors no longer have anything important to say that is worth listening to. In the case of senior women, we know we are not as physically agile as we once were and not many of us will run a marathon, but we *are* intellectually agile, alert and lively. We enjoy our interests and we enjoy other people and their interests. We feel we still have a lot to offer.

Seniors are here to stay! In fact, with the "Baby Boomers," our senior numbers are growing as well as the number of assisted living facilities and nursing homes being built all over America. Many new as well as older seniors would say that they still lead productive lives. In some cultures, seniors are greatly admired and sought out by the young to share their knowledge and wisdom gained through life and career experiences. Seniors in America and throughout the world can still have significant purpose.

And, God Himself verifies that truth for senior women in His Scripture: The Book of Titus reveals that the *'older women should teach the younger women'*. (See Titus 2:3-5.) Unfortunately, we do not usually hear that from our church pulpits. We are not encouraged to believe that God will help us grow to our full potential and find

His plan and purpose for our lives—no matter what our age—so we can, in turn, teach and encourage younger women to hope in Christ and His Word. Therefore, many of us women cannot imagine that God could still use us in a dynamic way late in our lives. I know for a fact that God will, indeed, use us—whatever our age, race, ethnicity, marital status or social-economic position—for His purpose.

A good example is a woman named Della, who is a personal friend of mine. After retirement as a college professor, Della joined *The Peace Corps* and served in China for many of her elder years. Eventually, a woman witnessed Christ and shared Bible truth with her. At the age of 85, she received *the promise of new life* to be born again of the Spirit—fulfilling her long search for the true meaning and purpose for her life. With that, she had the fire of the Spirit burning within her to serve God. She returned to the United States with renewed energy and vitality and God, indeed, opened to her a ministry to serve Him. Through Della's witness for Christ and her biblical teachings, the Lord brought many people into *the promise of new life* to be born again of the Spirit. It's never too late.

Something to consider is that without knowledge of the Bible and God's promises offered to all believers, we might find that we are spiritually living far below the expectations God has for us. On a personal note, I know that despite the fact that I believed, prayed, and attended church for thirty years of my life, I was living far below God's expectations and purpose for me. Why? Because I was ignorant of the Holy Scriptures and what God says about me as His daughter, and what He promises He will do for me and give to me. It was not until I received *God's answer, the promise of new life* in Christ and was born again of the Spirit that I learned and believed who I was in God, and began walking the path that led me into His plan and His expectations. Studying the Bible, with the Holy Spirit supernaturally opening my understanding and revealing truth to me, was what caused me—and causes me to this day—to continue seeking to learn God's marvelous, miraculous ways. However, please know that none of this comes to a believer without being tested by trials, through which we learn to trust God. And trusting God is what causes us to *thrive* and grow in the midst of our trials, so that we have a "testimony" to His glory. No *test*, no *testimony!* Gratefully, I learned early in my *new life* with Christ, that the Bible is God's *love letter* to each of us, individually; but it is also His *Handbook* to instruct and teach us how we can successfully live His expectations not only for our spiritual life but also, for our everyday practical life.

So, what do women want? Wherever we are spiritually, we have to admit that we all have the same basic needs. What do we *really* want and need on a personal level? I have learned over the many years of my public ministry to women, that whatever we consider our life condition and circumstances to be—whether ideal, tolerable, challenging or extreme—wherever we are spiritually and whether or not we are a churchgoer—each of us wants to be the best woman we can be in every area of our life. As stated before, we women have a deep yearning to be valued, loved, accepted, appreciated, wanted, needed, and to have purpose in our life. We are all the same. Some of us think of those *wants* as emotional needs, but I have learned that in reality, they are also spiritual needs.

For many of us, without having God at the center of our lives, we are desperate to find ways to fill the void in whatever areas we are lacking to make us feel better about ourselves and to feel our life has purpose. The more fortunate among us are in a position to find satisfaction and fulfillment in a larger variety of ways.

Each year millions of dollars are spent to buy the self-help books flooding the market for women to help us gain knowledge in the areas of self-discovery, self-improvement, mental and emotional health and physical fitness—all of which are written, in essence, to teach us: "Look your best, do your best, and be your best." I believe God wants that for us, too. However, while many of us do work hard at the physical as well as the mental and emotional aspects of our lives, we tend to neglect the spiritual part, which is the very component that can give us what we want—and bring us the help we need to find the balance in our lives we are looking for. Nonetheless, the time and effort spent to learn how to "look our best, do our best, and be our best"—can be a good thing. But God desires *more* for us.

Some of us find satisfaction and fulfillment In doing good works. We become volunteers in our communities, using our intelligence, talents and skills and faithfully giving many hours of service to charitable health organizations, hospitals, and elder care facilities. We promote various endeavors like the arts, historic restoration, politics or raising public awareness for other worthy causes. We join women's movements to campaign for the rights of children, the elderly, animals, the environment, and our equal rights to men in the job market. All of these *good works* benefit society and make for an important contribution of our time and efforts. Think about it. What would our American way of life be like without those of us who are volunteers? Because of us, the world is made a better place for everyone. Volunteering can be a good thing. But God desires *more* for us.

Others of us who are faithful church-going women, busy ourselves with church-related activities that satisfy emotional needs as well as allowing us to believe we are pleasing God and other people. Think about it. Most established churches could not function as well as they do without the work of *helps* done by those of us women who are members. Our time and efforts are well spent in this way. That can be a good thing, too. But God desires *more* for us.

Then there are those of us who seek more education through self-study for personal growth or university studies to prepare for a new career to elevate our income and station in life—enabling us to feel good about ourselves because we're moving toward a better lifestyle. That is also a good thing. But God desires *more* for us.

Or some of us just go shopping for shoes or sheets. We make a project out of updating our wardrobes or our homes. If we have an adequate budget that, too, can be a good thing. But God desires *more* for us.

None of these works are pointed out because they are bad in and of themselves—on the contrary. Whatever our efforts to better our communities and churches or to better ourselves—whether they appear serious or frivolous to others—we do whatever it takes to make us feel good about ourselves, to feel productive, and to feel we have purpose. The important thing for us to see is that these efforts *are* commendable. They do give us a sense of accomplishment, contribution, and a measure of success and personal fulfillment. Doing *good works,* living a good life, gaining more education, achieving success, and even making our homes and our wardrobes more attractive or improving our lives in any other way—is a good thing. The sad part of it is that some of us believe this is as good as life gets. As a result, by being satisfied with "good" it is possible for us to miss the "best," which I believe is what God desires for us.

However, we cannot forget that there are those who are much less fortunate as they live in extreme circumstances. Their life condition and problems are not only challenging but also, in some cases, they are cruelly severe and even debilitating. Nonetheless these women also long to "look their best, do their best, and be their best." They too, long to be valued, loved, accepted, appreciated, wanted, needed, and to have purpose for their lives. But the cards of life have been stacked against them. They used to be resilient. They could cope and make the most of their hard circumstances, but they no longer have that same resiliency they once had. They have been beaten down by life. Because of their extreme circumstances caused by their own bad choices or imposed on them by another, they live with constant emotional pain, struggle and hardship. They have lost their sense of self and value, and live with feelings of inadequacy and unworthiness. The dregs of their daily living absorb their waking thoughts, haunt their nights, and steal much of their energy—leaving them worn out and worn down. They cannot force themselves to rise above their heartaches of shattered dreams to achieve personal fulfillment. They are without hope. They have no more confidence that life can be better for them. They see no way out of the deep, dark pit of their extreme circumstances and can manage only to get by a day at a time. I know from personal experience that God definitely desires *more* for them.

Whatever your condition in life and wherever you are spiritually, I tell you on the authority of God's Word that He loves you unconditionally. In fact, if you did not rise above your current condition in life; if you did not live a good life; if you did not do good works; if you did not achieve to a level of success; if you did nothing remarkable; if you did nothing worthy of praise from God or people, He would love you just the same. Also, the fact is, the Bible makes clear that you cannot live in a pit of extreme circumstances too deep that God cannot reach down and pull you out to give you His *promise of new life*. On the other hand, you cannot live a good enough life;

you cannot be religious enough, attend church often enough or do enough *good works* for your community, church and others; nor can you perform well enough in your life or achieve enough success to deserve *the promise of new life*.

Unlike those in theater arts who can earn an Oscar, an Emmy or a Golden Globe for outstanding performance, *new life* in Christ can never be earned. So, if all your efforts cannot earn for you this "best" life God desires for you and you can never deserve it; where does that leave you? It leaves you right where you need to be—dependent upon a "higher power" to freely give you what you cannot earn. I believe that *higher power* is the only true and ever-living Jesus Christ. And, *the promise of new life* to be born again of the Spirit, is the "more" that God desires for you and me—and all people.

Now, you might be wondering, "If I choose *the promise of new life* in Christ, does that mean the experiences of my *old life* will have counted for nothing?" The resounding answer is, "No." God will use your past experiences; and He will use your intelligence, talents and skills; your hands-on ability as a volunteer in your church or community; your education; and your acquired career expertise. He will also use your difficult struggles, hardships and sufferings. It all counts to God.

That absolute claim is based upon my own personal experience after Jesus Christ rescued me from the extreme circumstances in which I once lived. The following scriptural promise proved true in my *new life*: "And we know that all things work together for good to those that love God, to them who are called according to *His* purpose" (Rom. 8:28). That means the *bad things* as well as the *good things* in your past, in your present, and in your future. This is an awesome promise of God, and I can testify that it is exciting when personally experienced. I have found that all of our life experiences come into play after receiving *the promise of new life*. In many cases, the experiences of our past unknowingly have perfectly prepared us for the specific plan and purpose God had designed for us to live out.

Although Sigmund Freud searched for thirty years, he did not find the answer to his question: What do women want? You have learned that God has always known what we women want. And, now you know *God's answer* and the *deep spiritual significance* it holds for all of us. The question remains: What do *you* want for *your* life?

I hope to persuade you to believe that by choosing *God's answer,* you are choosing the *first* of God's promises, *the promise of new life* to be born again of the Spirit, which is the "key" to receiving all of God's other promises made available to you in the Bible. The Holy Scriptures will help you live the *empowered life*—the life God had in mind for you when He created the unique woman you are. It will be different from any other woman's spiritual life, in the sense that it will be a life custom-made for you—to include your personality, gifts and specific skills. God's Word will not only teach you how to live your *new life* in Christ but also, how to live your everyday practical life. The Word of God has the power to keep you mentally, emotionally, and spiritually balanced. And yes, you will definitely feel valued, loved, accepted, appreciated, wanted, needed, and have purpose in your life. That is when you will discover for yourself that the Bible is the best *all-in-one* self-discovery, self-improvement, mental and emotional health and physical fitness book you will ever read to teach you how to *'Look your best, do your best and, be your best'*.

Some of you might be thinking this is all too good to be true and wondering, "Can all of this really be possible for me?" My answer is unequivocally, "Yes, it is all possible for you." Stay with me through the next chapter and together we will explore more Bible truth that will give you absolute assurance. I feel certain that *The Christian Factor* will help each of us examine ourselves even more closely to know where we are spiritually and to determine exactly where we want to be.

Chapter Three

THE CHRISTIAN FACTOR: WHAT IS A BORN AGAIN CHRISTIAN?

W e covered a lot of information in *The Woman Factor,* about embracing *the promise of new life* in Christ to become born again of the Spirit and *empowered,* and what that can mean to those of us who are *God-seeking women.* Therefore, I trust that all of us are now ready to explore in detail, *The Christian Factor.*

Let us begin with basic Bible truth to learn what being "Christian" is all about. Just to be certain we are all on the same page, we will start by looking at the fundamental beliefs of the Christian faith. The "Cliff Notes" version goes like this:

God created everything, including mankind, and saw that it was good. He placed Adam and Eve in the Garden and told them they could eat from every tree except "The Tree of Life." Satan came along and convinced them that they could defy God and eat from *The Tree of Life* and they would end up with wisdom just like God and be better off. So, they believed the lie, and did eat from the forbidden *Tree.* As a result, they were thrown into a "fallen" spiritual state whereby their nature became sinful. As punishment, they were banished from the Garden, and God relegated them to a life of hard work and pain. (See Gen. 3:23.)

Then God provided the "Law" of the Old Testament that in effect, basically, taught man: If you can keep all of these commands, you can be saved from your sinful self. Time proved that not one, not even the most pious and sincere, could keep all of the commandments, because of their sin nature. The Lord saw that the wickedness of man was great; and brought forth the flood as a new beginning. Although He allowed people to sacrifice animals whose shed blood would atone for their sins; still, the people waxed more and more evil and rebellious against God. And since spiritual death was the punishment for sin against God, all of mankind deserved to die and go to hell, where they would be forever separated from God.

But, God loved mankind and wanted us to be in fellowship with Him now and eternally—so much so, that He sent to earth His only begotten Son, Jesus Christ, the Messiah, to be the Savior of all mankind. Jesus was born of a virgin to live as fully God and fully man; and He would show mankind by example and teaching how we could live our best life in His power of love, peace, joy, health, and prosperity. But our sin debt needed to be paid for us to enjoy that privilege—and the only adequate payment was the shedding of totally innocent blood.

Therefore, Jesus, who was the only sinless One, took upon Himself all of our sins and willingly paid our sin debt in full by being crucified on a cross and dying in our place. He was buried, and on the third day he miraculously arose from the grave, defeating sin and death; and he was seen by hundreds of people before ascending back to His Father in Heaven. The shed blood of Jesus was the ultimate sacrifice. God the Father declared that forever there would be no other blood sacrifice needed to cover man's sin and reconcile him to God. That could only be possible through Jesus, who is the only "Mediator" between God and man. And all any of us would need to do from then on was believe in our hearts that Jesus is, indeed, God's Son and by His shed blood, death, and resurrection alone, our sins would be covered—forgiven—then we would receive *the promise of new life* to be reconciled to God. If we did believe, along with our *new life*, God would give us a new nature to enable us to fellowship with Him here on earth and then, to spend eternity with Him in heaven.

There is much more rich scriptural truth to share, but in short, that is the essential Bible truth of the Christian faith. At first, this might seem to read more like a fantasy than the Christian doctrine that it is. If that is the case with you, know that you wouldn't be the first person to feel that way, but later to believe, by faith, that it is absolutely true and life changing.

However, we must understand that believing it, is not just *intellectually* believing in a "Creed," but it is believing with our heart in a "Person"—the *Person* of Jesus, The Christ, who alone can save us from our sins. We, as all humanity, face the same dilemma: We all know we have sinned and understand that without Christ's forgiveness and cleansing from our sins, we cannot be in relationship with our Holy God. Further, we must have a "heart experience" according to Scripture. That is, we have to set aside our pride, admit we are a sinner and that we need Christ to forgive our sins, so we can be connected to the Living God and fellowship with Him. We all must make our own choice to accept or reject this foundational Bible belief of Christ's sacrifice on the cross to be reconciled to our Creator, our Heavenly Father.

Not everyone has heard this Bible account of what it means to be a Christian. On the other hand, the great tragedy is that many *have* heard this biblical truth and have rejected it. Some are like the "rich young ruler" Scripture tells about, who placed his trust in material possessions and turned his back on the real truth. (See Matt. 19.) In fact, many are actually hostile to what the Bible teaches. Others have refused to even listen.

Despite the knowledge of the Bible available to people today, while many are not opposed to Christ or Christianity, without knowing what the Bible says, they have their own concept for what Christian means. Each of us is, indeed, free to choose what we believe. Many believe they are Christian because they faithfully attend church and practice religious traditions; and others believe they are going to heaven because they live a moral life and do good deeds. Some believe that all religious doctrines point to the same God; and that there are *different paths* to God. Others are convinced that there is more than one way and there are many *options* from which to choose how they can *know* God.

While I respect people who hold these personal views and the sincerity of what they believe, the Bible will prove them to be sincerely wrong. The truth is, that it is not what *we* think and say is the acceptable *path* to God or the *way* to know God in order to enjoy a true relationship with Him and be assured of eternal life; but it is what *God* thinks and says in His written Word, the Holy Bible, that counts. It is the only source of the doctrine of the resurrected Jesus Christ whom Scripture describes as God, who came in the flesh: "For in Christ lives all the fullness of God in a human body" (Col. 2:9, NLT).

Be assured that God the Father loves each individual unconditionally, regardless of his or her personal views. But, that doesn't change the fact that the Lord Jesus, Himself said, "And this is eternal life, that they might know Thee, the only true God, and Jesus Christ whom Thou hast sent" (John 17:3).

Since I have already established that the Bible is my standard for truth and final authority to know God and to have eternal life, I will show you more specifically by Scripture how we can have our sin debt paid in full by believing there is only "one way" to God the Father and that is through His Only Begotten Son, Jesus, the Christ. It is written:

- "Jesus, said... I am the way, the truth, and the life: no man comes to the Father, but by Me" (John 14:6).
- "And the Word was made flesh, and dwelt among us, and we beheld his glory, the glory as of the only begotten of the Father, full of grace and truth" (John 1:14).
- "For in Him *(Jesus)* the whole fullness of Deity (the Godhead) continues to dwell in bodily form [giving complete expression of the divine nature]" (Col.2:9, Italics added, AMP).
- Speaking of Jesus: "The great *and* important *and* weighty, we confess, is the hidden truth (the mystic secret) of godliness. He [God] was made visible in human flesh" (I Tim. 3:16a, AMP).
- "There is salvation in no one else! God has given no other name *(except Jesus)* under heaven by which we must be saved" (Acts 4:12, NLT, Italics added).

45

- "For there is one God, and one mediator between God and men, the man Christ Jesus; who gave Himself a ransom for all... " (I Tim. 2:5-6, NKJ, Greek NT, and Douay versions).

These Scriptures confirm Jesus alone has the preeminence as the "One Mediator" between man and God the Father. It is a foundational truth to which all followers of Christ testify. By their own experience they have found there is, indeed, only *one mediator* and only *one way* to God and that is through Jesus Christ, the Son of God and the true Messiah.

In addition to the above Scriptures, let us look at other Scriptures that confirm and establish that the *one way* we can ever hope to see and enter the kingdom of God is to be born again—and how we can experience it:

- "Jesus replied, "I tell you the truth, unless you are born again, you cannot see the Kingdom of God" (John 3:3, NLT).
- "So don't be surprised when I say, You must be born again" (John 3:7, NLT, NKJ, Greek NT, and Douay Versions).
- "All praise to God, the Father of our Lord Jesus Christ. It is by His great mercy that we have been born again, because God raised Jesus Christ from the dead" (I Peter 1:3, NLT).
- "For you have been born again, but not to a life that will quickly end. Your new life will last forever because it comes from the eternal, living word of God" (I Peter 1:23, NLT).
- "If you confess with your mouth that Jesus is Lord and believe in your heart that God raised him from the dead, you will be saved. For it is by believing in your heart that you are made right with God, and it is by confessing with your mouth that you are saved" (Rom. 10:9-10, NLT).
- "Repent therefore and be converted, that your sins may be blotted out, so that times of refreshing may come from the presence of the Lord" (Acts 3:19, NKJV).

Now that we have reviewed the fundamental faith or belief that defines *Christian* and the specific Scriptures verifying by what means we can be reconciled to God the Father, I trust that we all agree that the Bible clearly states that there is only *one way* to know God, to have our sins forgiven, to have eternal life, and to have an ongoing, authentic relationship with Him. That way is through faith in Jesus Christ, His sacrifice on the cross, and according to His own spoken words recorded in the Bible: "You must be born again" (John 3:7).

When we choose to take this step, we will know we are connected to the true and Living God. It is an amazing fact, that when we *believe,* we definitely know we have had a "heart experience" with Christ. That is paramount. It is only then we know we have been *empowered.* He empowers us by sending His Holy Spirit to live in our hearts—and we will never be the same.

After acting by faith on what we believe with our heart, as it is written, we will know we have been: "Born again of not corruptible seed, but of the incorruptible (seed) of the Word of God, which liveth and abideth forever" (I Peter 1:23). Our heart is forever changed. In other words, "It is no longer I who live, but Christ lives in me" (Gal. 2: 20, NLT).

Regardless of our prior religious orientation and on what basis we previously defined ourselves as being Christian, we must understand that the Holy Scriptures must always take precedence over our personal experience and the word of man. If our experience and man's word is of God, it will line up with what God's Word says. We are not to judge the Bible; but rather, the Bible judges us.

You might be wondering what comes next. First of all, know that when we have become born again according to Scripture, we can be certain that we are *empowered.* At this point, with our activated faith in Jesus Christ and His Word, the Holy Spirit will begin to teach us through the Bible, who we are to God and how He sees us. We will discover that we were "chosen" by God (Psalm 139). We will now understand that *God first loved us.* The Bible will make clear that God gave us the desire to be His—even before we were conscious of our own desire to know Him. Then He gave us an ear to hear Bible truth and our faith to believe it. God gave us the grace to turn from our sin and want to change. And God will place in our path the right people of influence for Christ to help us grow. Remarkable!

When I look back on my own experience, I realize prior to each step I took toward my first encounter with Christ, just the right person had been placed in my path to share her testimony and speak Bible truth to me; then the same thing happened as God moved me along to take my next step in Christ, and the next step. God has always used people of influence for Christ in my path to help me grow in faith and fulfill His plan—and I treasure each person who was used of God in this way to bless my life.

Also, now born again, we will learn from the Bible that God intends our life to be successful and fruitful in every aspect. But our success and fruitfulness in all things will only come by planting the seeds of God's Word in our heart. All of this is a benefit of receiving *the promise of new life*. Then, transformation will begin for each of us to become the woman God created us to be. It is all pretty amazing, I know.

You probably think that all of this sounds too good to be true. You are right. In the natural it is. Making a decision to submit one's self wholly in faith to become born again is an amazing, supernatural one-time experience—but that is just the beginning. Even though Jesus does meet us right where we are to give us our *new life* in Him, He does not expect us to stay that way. We cannot begin our Christian walk by being satisfied with the way we are or comparing ourselves with anyone else, because we will judge ourselves to be either better or worse.

If we want to grow in our faith to receive all of God's promises and to live the successful or fruitful life—the *empowered,* abundant life—the only standard of perfection to which we should compare ourselves is the character of Jesus. He desires to conform us to His image and become all He intends for us to be. Only exposure to the Bible will *mirror* the true image of *who* we really are. In order to be all God promises we can be, we will recognize that we, indeed, need to be transformed.

I learned this after having become born again and studying the Bible for the first time. I came to complete brokenness and humility when I saw myself in the "mirror" of God's Word, and surrendered to its transforming power. With the help of the Holy Spirit within, I will-ingly removed the mask I had previously been wearing for so many years to disguise my pain, and to defend and protect my image to the world. We all need to see our own reflection in the *mirror* of the Bible's perfect revelation of who Jesus is and what His true followers really look like. The power to make all of that happen comes by exercising our faith in God's Word. However, even when we have a heart that desires to be transformed by God's Word, walking it out in real time and living it is always harder—but not impossible.

By now some of us might be scratching our heads and wondering, "Can all of that really happen for me?" That answer comes with a simple question: God has given His life for us, so will we trust God enough to surrender our life to Him? Surrendering our life to God might be a little scary since we have always been in control of it, but it is in our best interest to do so. That is what God is waiting for. It will take our steadfast, immovable faith and complete trust in Christ and His Word to believe the truth of the Bible, as we read and study it. The Scriptures will renew our mind and transformation will begin to change different aspects of our life, whether or not we were previously aware that those changes were needed. Transformation will come by also desiring God to change our negative habits, which we might have previously tried to change many times, but were unsuccessful. Once we embrace our *new life* in Christ, the power of God the Holy Spirit is actively working within to help us make those changes.

God's Word will change our personality and behavior wherever needed; such as, our thought life, emotions, desires, motives, attitudes, actions and reactions as well as our sins of pride, self-righteousness, presumption, and judging—bringing our overall character and conduct into alignment with God's character traits which controlled His behavior when He walked the earth; namely: "Love, joy, peace, patience, kindness, goodness, faithfulness, gentleness, and self-control" (Gal. 5:22). The Bible describes these character traits of God as "fruit of the Spirit," which was the core, the essence of Jesus' personality.

By our daily yielding to the Holy Spirit within, God will develop His character and conduct—His "fruit"—in each of us by His power, so we can successfully live our *new life* with God and man. Little by little our personality will change to reflect the character of Jesus, the *fruit of the Spirit*. Also this will govern our behavior when interacting with our spouses, children, relatives, friends, neighbors, co-workers, fellow Christians, those of other religious persuasions, and all other people—helping us do our part in keeping our relationships in harmony. These developed traits will bring God's intended fruitfulness into all aspects of our living. However, in order for that to happen, it requires not only our total surrender but also, inviting God the Holy Spirit to intervene in every aspect of our personal life to bring effective transformation.

There is no exact pattern or formula that can be given for this transformation. We are each unique and only God knows the changes needed and how He can bring them about. The Bible makes clear that it will take our cooperation with God the Holy Spirit in order to do it. Again, as we fully yield to Jesus and His Word, the Holy Spirit will take the lead. However, there is no such thing as being perfect just because we are born again. Perfection will not come until we get to heaven. In this life we will always be a work in progress. Therefore, in a weak moment we may fail. But we know if we immediately repent, God is faithful to forgive us—and once again, we will do our best to let the *fruit of the Spirit* rule in us.

From personal experience I can give this assurance: If we do yield or surrender to Christ and His Word, we will find that these traits or the *fruit of the Spirit* developing in us will help us function in a more healthy way in every area of our life. The Bible declares: "For God has not given us a spirit of fear, but of power and of love and a sound mind" (2 Tim. 1:7, NKJV).

Since our body is a responder to our mental, emotional, and spiritual health and we are now living a peaceful, stress-free life and adhering to the Bible as our *all-in-one* greatest Source for self-discovery, self-improvement, mental, emotional, spiritual, and physical fitness—we will, indeed, *'look our best, do our best, and be our best'*, no matter what age we are and even in the midst of our trials and sufferings.

In order for this to happen, however, we must believe that there is power in the Bible that is capable of helping us to achieve this. We must believe that the Bible is the inspired Word of God. "In the beginning before all time was the Word (Christ), and the Word was with God, and the Word was God Himself... And the Word (Christ) became flesh and lived among us... ." (See John 1:1-14, AMP.)

If we will believe in the power of God's Word, the Bible will help us to improve our life in every area of our daily practical living. The Bible has the supernatural power to help us do everything we need to do in order to live a happy, peaceful, stress-free life. In addition to all we have shared that the Bible will do, it also has the power to deliver us from tormenting fears of all kinds or demonic oppression, and it will free us from our secret weaknesses. The Bible will heal our relationships; and it will help us to be an even better wife, mother, sister, grandmother, friend, neighbor, employee or employer—whatever applies to us. Overall, the Bible will build up our personhood, our self-esteem, and our self-confidence. Also, it will help us to see our purpose as a witness for Christ—and to fulfill it. The Bible's principles will counsel and guide us to make wise decisions, which will benefit us as well as our loved ones. The Bible will develop, expand, and mature our faith to believe God for all of His promises by which He wants His children to benefit. The Bible will make us content and happy. Everything we will ever need and everything we will ever receive from God will be manifested according to our faith, His Word and His All-knowing Will for our lives. The Bible will cause us to thrive in our trials and triumph in our endeavors.

Also, the Bible makes clear that if we surrender ourselves and our future to Jesus as we follow Him day-by-day, not only will we find we have been transformed in personality and conduct but also, the Holy Spirit will begin orchestrating our life. With our trust and cooperation, God will lead us into the future He already had planned for us. We might not understand everything He is doing to bring that about, but God clearly promises in His Word: "We are assured and know that God being a partner in their labor, all things work together and are fitting into a plan for good to and for those who love God and are called according to His design and purpose" (Rom. 8:28, AMP).

It bears emphasizing that transformation will not happen instantaneously, but will only happen by cultivating a consistent relationship with Jesus Christ and through our dependence on Him and His Word. We will find that transformation is, in reality, a life-long process. But by inviting God to orchestrate our life, the power of the Holy Spirit within will, indeed, change us and get us to that place God has planned for us as the Bible declares: "Eye has not seen and ear has not heard and has not entered into the heart of men, all that God has prepared for those who love Him, who hold Him in affectionate reverence, promptly obeying Him and gratefully recognizing the benefits He has bestowed" (I Cor. 2:9, AMP).

God will use each of us believers in our individual corner of the world, to show His love to and for those who do not yet know Him. When we are a believer who is born again of the Spirit according to Jesus' own words in John 3: 1-7, we will be a good witness for Christ as a member of any Bible-believing church.

As if all of the above were not enough to get our faith engine revved up, we also can look forward to the Holy Spirit empowering and enabling us with abilities to do more than we imagined ourselves capable, and over and above all that we had ever dreamed possible. The Bible declares: "Now to him who... by the power that is at work within us, is able to carry out His purpose and do superabundantly, far over and above all that we dare ask or think [infinitely beyond our highest prayers, desires, thoughts, hopes or dreams]" (Eph. 3:20, AMP).

I have learned that there is no intimate relationship with Christ; no permanent victory over fear, insecurities, weaknesses, habits and sins of the flesh; no enduring transformation, spiritual growth and maturity; no overcoming power of faith, trust, hope and peace to go through or overcome the hardships of life; no triumph in Christ, no longevity as a true follower of Christ—outside of what the Bible calls being "born again of the Spirit" and yielding to the Holy Spirit for transformation.

In the next two chapters we will meet some biblical characters whose stories are recorded for us—one from the Old Testament, and six others from the New Testament. They are all living *empowered* lives. We can learn from how God interacts with them and their obedience to all He teaches. From their extraordinary encounters they grew by faith in God's words and rose to their full potential and were *enabled* to live out God's plan and purpose for an *empowered* life. All of their stories will make clear that God is Sovereign. He has a unique plan for each of us that will help us live a better life than we could imagine for ourselves. He sees the heart of each individual in the human family. God knows and loves us unconditionally before we even have the desire to seek Him, to know Him or to love Him. We will find if we do seek Him with all our heart, He will also meet us in a unique way to give us *the promise of new* life to be born again of the Spirit and *empowered*.

Chapter Four

THE EMPOWERED FACTOR:
A BIBLICAL PROFILE OF AN
EMPOWERED WOMAN

J esus said, "I am come that they might have life, and that they might have it more abundantly" (John 10:10b). Let us consider how God sees all of us women and exactly how He expects us to live that "abundant life"—that *empowered* life He wants to give us.

By now, we should all be in agreement that every one of us women not only wants to feel *empowered* to deal with our trials but also, we want to *'look our best, do our best,* and *be our best'* and live the most fulfilling life we can. In fact, I believe God wants that for us even more than we want it for ourselves. As a brand new "born again of the Spirit" believer, I searched the Scriptures to find out how to be the best Christian I could be. Also, I wanted to be the best woman, wife, and mother I could be. But since I did not fit my own long-held perception of what a woman of God should be like and look like, I was not sure what God expected of me as a spiritual woman. I began listening to Christian radio preachers. The only thing I heard about a woman of God was that she should be "submissive to her husband" and that "she should fit in with her husbands plans." I believed that but also, I believed God gave us our *brain,* so I silently questioned: *Doesn't God expect us women to use our intelligence and abilities?* I heard no biblical teaching on that subject. In fact, I never heard anything else about women or what God expected a spiritual woman's demeanor to be.

If you have not searched the Bible on your own to learn how God sees a woman, you might believe as I did before learning the truth; that is, a spiritual woman, totally committed to God, would surely be rather docile, in the sense of being passive. And if married, she might be expected to be dependent on her husband to make every decision for her, for their family and for their home. Oh, and one more thing I was certain of, was that her whole life would be void of adornment of any kind—and dull. Her clothing would be without anything bright, cheerful and colorful—nothing pretty and pink and certainly not "stylish" clothing made from fine fabrics—nor would she care about "decorating" to make her home attractive. That image of a woman of God might seem to have been a silly one to some of you. Nevertheless, when I was a young girl that is what I thought a true woman of God must look like and be like.

Looking back, I wonder where that early perception came from. My own mother certainly had not fit that image. In fact, while she was a very good woman and an excellent wife, mother and home-maker—she also was *stylish,* talented, intelligent, and had a spirit of independence my father always seemed to respect and admire. Therefore, wherever my early image of a godly or spiritual woman came from—the time would come when I would learn it did not come from God.

Searching both my King James Bible and the family Catholic Douay Version of the Bible, which my mother gave me, I studied many women whose lives are recorded in both Bibles as well as everything God says about women. I discovered that the Apostle Paul wrote the Book of Titus, instructing Titus, one of his spiritual sons in the faith, to remain in Crete to teach the new followers of Christ how to live as Christians. When it came to women, Paul told him to "teach the older women to live in a way that honors God," and also, that "they should teach the younger women to love their husbands and their children, to live wisely and be pure, to work in their homes, to do good, and to be submissive to their husbands" (Titus 2:3-5a, NLT). That told me a lot, but I still wondered about a spiritual woman's appearance, mannerisms, character, conduct, and how she should use the intelligence and abilities she had been given. I determined to find out those answers.

It did not take long for me to recognize that there was much more written about women in God's Word than I had imagined. Then, in both Bible versions, I studied Proverbs 31 in detail. That's when my previous perception of a spiritual woman *began* changing. When I studied Proverbs 31 in my Amplified Bible, with its expanded meaning of certain words, that version gave me an even clearer understanding of God's profile of a spiritual woman. Now my previous perception was *completely* changed.

It was sheer pleasure for me to learn about the Proverbs 31 woman's private life, which was divinely inspired by God, Himself. Obviously, it had been written for me and for all women as an example of an *empowered* woman living an *abundant* life. Because God inspired this writing, we women can recognize our inherent value to God, and what He expects us to be like in character and conduct. And yes, I believe it was written to show us not only how we should behave but also, how we should *look* as His daughters— daughters of the King.

I think you will enjoy reading what I learned in my study about this woman. I was thrilled to discover that she was an altogether different kind of woman than my mind had perceived when I was young. I gleaned from my study that this woman was definitely not *docile* in the sense of being *passive,* and she definitely was not a wife who was dependent on her husband to make every decision for her as well as the family and their household. Actually, I found she was neither a "Pollyanna" nor a "Prima Dona"—and she definitely was not *plain, dowdy, dull* or uninteresting. I found her fascinating.

Because God, Himself, had inspired these Scriptures, when I studied that woman, I believed she was my example of what God intended me and every woman to be like when living to her full potential. I was thirty-years-old and had just begun to live my *new life* in Christ, and did not have a clue what my full potential could be. Nonetheless, I believed this Bible truth could shape my life if I put all my faith in God to help me develop to *my* full potential. I knew that meant more needed transformation, but I desired to be like that Proverbs 31 woman. My identification with her was because she, too, was a wife, mother and homemaker—and totally committed to her God. I saw her as an excellent example for me. In fact, I thought she was a woman with whom all 21st century women could identify, on one or more levels—regardless of marital status or religious persuasion. I am excited to share with you what I learned.

In capsule form, Proverbs 31 begins with the king's mother advising him in the first nine verses about how a young man should conduct himself and the kind of woman he should seek out for his wife. Then the king, in turn, passes on this advice in verses 10-31. These Scripture verses made clear to me *what* this woman was like and *how* she lived her life. Her identity was in God. I was convinced that she was a woman of God first—before a wife and helpmate, and a mother. Although she was "submissive" to her own husband, according to Scripture, it appeared to me that her *submission* was to God, first. Here are my conclusions about how these scriptures can apply to today's woman, including myself:

• God's description of this woman told me that she was an exceptional person. She was a woman with admirable traits; and she was a good wife to her husband just as Verses 10–12 describe her: *"She is a capable, intelligent, and virtuous woman... She is far more precious than jewels; her value is far above rubies or pearls... The heart of her husband trusts in her confidently and relies on and believes in her securely... She comforts, encourages, and does him only good as long as there is life in her."* Verse 23 makes clear that her husband was *"well-known in the gates (meaning the city)"* and he, obviously, trusted her to hold the family and home together while he was with *"the elders, the nobles, and the judges."*

In today's society her husband might be a Rabbi, Christian minister, politician, judge, lawyer, physician, teacher, janitor, truck driver, electrician, entrepreneur, corporate CEO or any other white-collar or equally important blue-collar gentleman—who is definitely *one of the good guys,* away from the house, working to make a living.

• She was always prepared for the changing seasons when it came to proper clothing for her and her family, as described in Verse 13: *"She seeks out wool and flax and works with willing hands to develop it"* and Verse 19 explains that *"she lays her hands to the spindle"* to weave cloth from which to sew items. Indeed she was a talented and hard-working woman because I learned she sewed all the clothing for her family. Moreover, Verse 22 reveals, *"Her clothing is of linen, pure and fine, and of silk and purple, such as that of which the clothing of the priests and the hallowed cloths of the temple were made."* In other words, her own clothing fabrics were the more exquisite, quality fabrics, and purple was a color identified with royalty. She was not pretentious but, obviously, she liked the "finer" things—and, apparently, her husband could afford to buy those more extravagant, elegant fabrics from which she sewed her own clothing. In addition, she was no doubt interested in interior decorating to create an attractive home, because I also learned in Verse 22 that *"She makes for herself coverlets, cushions, and rugs of tapestry."*

In today's society, many women might not know how to design and sew *'clothing'* for themselves and their family or *'coverlets, cushions and rugs of tapestry'* for their homes as the Proverbs 31 woman did. Some of us women do sew clothing and make decorative items for our homes; but the majority of women buy those items. Nonetheless, either way, women today know how to make a house a home—whether on a large or a limited budget. They, like the Proverbs 31 woman, make sure that they and their families are properly clothed for all seasons, and that their homes are attractive.

• She ran her household with ease. In fact, Verse 15 told me that *"She rises while it is yet night... and assigns her maids their tasks."*

Today's woman might not have household help. Nonetheless, she knows what it is to rise before dawn to prepare for the day: to get her family off to work and school before she begins her long workday, with household duties that can sometimes continue into the night; especially so, if she also has outside employment.

• She's described in Verse 17 like this: *"She girds herself with strength [spiritual, mental, and physical fitness for her God-given tasks] and makes her arms strong and firm."* Obviously, she spent priority time with her God for spiritual and mental strength—and she exercised.

Today's woman not only spends private or group time in prayer and Bible study, growing in spiritual knowledge and wisdom but also, she uses her intelligence and capabilities to be a help to her husband, and to take care of family and home responsibilities. She takes charge of her own health by exercising or working out at home or going to a fitness center.

• She was obviously interested in commerce as well as being industrious and gifted with creativity, according to Verse 24: *"She makes fine linen garments to sell in the marketplace; she delivers to the merchants girdles for sashes"*—no doubt to bring extra income into the household. In other words, she had *savoir-faire*. She must have been knowledgeable about marketing the homemade items she sold. All of that is pretty impressive.

Today's woman might be savvy in the same way and with those abilities she might be a dress designer; a marketing executive for one of the top fabric or clothing manufactures; or she might own a retail clothing store in her town. Come to think of it, she might even run a cottage industry from her home to make extra money for her household.

• She had a positive outlook on life, as Verse 25 told me: *"Strength and dignity are her clothing and her position is strong and secure; she rejoices over the future… [knowing that she and her family are in readiness for it]!"* Clearly this woman was a fantastic household manager and knew how to plan for the needs of her family and home—even on the chance of an unforeseen disaster. I have to believe, she was the one in a crowd whose positive attitude encouraged and brought out the best in others and made them feel good about themselves and more optimistic about their own futures.

In today's society, all of us women could take a lesson from this woman to try harder to keep a positive attitude even in the face of our many challenges. Sometimes that is easier said than done, but not impossible, if we are God-conscious in our daily lives and adhering to Bible principles. There is, seemingly, no easy solution to the problems women and their families are dealing with in this current economy and cultural environment. But suffice it to say, we might all find that if we put the full weight of our problems on God and trust Him, as the Proverbs 31 woman clearly did, we will feel more positive and secure, too—and we will get through these tough times. That is not just rhetoric on my part. I can say it because I have learned to practice it to the best of my ability—and it has proven true for me.

• She was a woman with wisdom and self-control. Whenever she interacted with others, Verse 26 describes her this way: *"She opens her mouth in skillful and godly wisdom, and on her tongue is the law of kindness [giving counsel and instruction]."*

Today's woman, who is intelligent as well as wise in her counsel and instruction like the Proverbs 31 woman, might apply her developed skills as a teacher, social worker, office manager, corporate CEO, physician, lawyer, a congresswoman or as governor of her state. Just as impressive, kindness would be on her lips when interacting with people in her workplace, community, and church; with her family and relatives—and even at the kitchen table in a conversation with her best friend who is sharing her troubled heart and asking her advice.

• She paid attention to what was happening with her husband and children as Verse 27 told me *"She looks well to how things go in her household."* That same verse also went on to tell me that she was a woman not given to *"idleness" (gossip, discontent, and self-pity),"* which told me that if she had a bad day, she did not feel sorry for herself and have a pity-party or complain about it to everyone. Nor was she nosey or a busybody, who sought after *ripe* and *juicy* gossip about the lives of other people and talked about them to everyone else. In other words, she minded her own business.

In today's society, I considered this Scripture was telling me that I, and may I suggest most women, would do ourselves a favor to learn and practice this woman's way of disciplining herself. Ouch! Also that I, and women in general, would do well to avoid the temptation to get wrapped-up in the negatives of life, but rather remove ourselves as much as possible, from idle gossip in the office or among friends—in order to stay focused on the positive.

• She was a benevolent woman, as I learned when reading Verse 20: *"She opens her hand to the poor, yes she reaches out her filled hand to the needy."*

Today's woman might not be able to literally reach out with *'her filled hand to the needy'*. But she might be able to financially support her church and charitable outreaches, which do benefit the less fortunate or serve as a volunteer for the Red Cross, The Salvation Army, Catholic Charities, a nursing home, a food bank or other benevolent organizations.

• She was evidently a good mother, parenting her children with love and, no doubt, teaching and disciplining them according to God's principles, because Verse 28 declares, *"Her children rise up and call her blessed."*

Today's woman tries to be a good mother, too. Ideally, we show our love to our children by our words and actions and make each one feel secure and an important member of the family. We teach them godly principles, responsibility, good hygiene, and good manners. We also teach them to have self-respect and respect for others as well as respect for authority—and other things too numerous to mention here. In this 24-hour-a-day-job, we cannot forget "discipline," the other side of the joys of mothering; and hopefully, always balanced with "love." We have all made mistakes; and there is always room for us to learn and improve. But, if we have *mothered* our children to the best of our ability, then like the Proverbs 31 woman, we can hope our children will also *'rise up and call us blessed'*.

• She was a keen-minded decision-maker as Verse 16 told me: *"She considers a new field before she buys or accepts it."* So, she not only had the intelligence but, obviously, she also had the wisdom and discernment to appraise the property, evaluate its worth and negotiate the price. Then she had the confidence to transact the purchase. Moreover, it is made clear that she bought that piece of real estate on her own.

In today's society, a woman with that same keen-minded decision-making, wise negotiating skills, and confidence would be able to fully participate in every area of decision making to run her household and even make major purchases on her own to benefit her family. With those same abilities, she is not only able to purchase property, but she might even own the real estate company. Or, with the same level of skill and proficiency that the Proverbs 31 woman possessed, today's woman actually can do just about anything she sets her mind to—even head up a Fortune 500 company. This is a woman who might, along with her husband, have an interest in building financial security and, therefore, she is an avid viewer of *The Suze Orman Show* on TV, where she learns all she can about saving and investing their finances.

• She was strong. The second part of Verse 16 told me that with her physical strength, "She plants fruitful vines in her vineyard"—no doubt, in that same field she purchased. Imagine!

Today's woman might plant her own vegetable garden to help feed her family organic meals or her hobby might be flower gardening. It takes physical strength to do both. Or, with her *know-how*, diligence, and strength she can competently operate her own nursery business.

• She did not get her value from her husband—she got her value from God. Nonetheless, I found that her husband did highly value her as Verses 28 and 29 revealed his pride in her: *"Her husband boasts of and praises her, saying 'Many daughters (of God) have done virtuously, nobly, and well, with the strength of character that is steadfast in goodness, but you excel them all'."*

In today's society, any woman would be thrilled to hear that kind of praise from her husband.

• Clearly, the secret to this woman's success in living her best life, the *abundant life* God *empowered* and enabled her to live, is found in Verse 30: *"Charm is deceptive and beauty is vain and does not last* (even for Miss Universe), *but a woman who reverently fears the Lord will be praised."*

In today's culture, which concentrates so much on outward appearances, we would all be wiser to focus more on our inner beauty, which comes from a reverent fear of the Lord. That way, we might also feel a lot more secure.

• God's description of His *empowered* woman ends by making clear what this woman's reward was for living her life under the influence of God, in Verse 31: *"Give her the fruit of her hands and let her own works praise her"* (See Pro. 31, AMP).

I am sure you realize as I do, that this woman was amazing. Perfection! Obviously, she represents a woman who pleases God. There is no doubt that this woman of God had developed to her full potential and was definitely living the *abundant life*.

These Scriptures *blew to smithereens* my long-held perception of a spiritual woman. This Proverbs 31 woman was anything but passive, plain, uninteresting, or dominated by her husband. Indeed, she was a woman who had found *God's answer* for her life. She definitely was a liberated woman who, we can assume, lived her life in total freedom. She was a God-fearing, God-influenced, well-balanced woman, who was *empowered* and enabled by the Holy Spirit in her daily living, and she knew her value in God. She had the confidence to use her intelligence, creative abilities and all the other skills God equipped her with not only to help her family but also, to feel good about herself, to feel productive, and to know her life had purpose. She pleased God and her life blessed her family and others. I believe the Proverbs 31 woman was included in the Bible to show women of past generations as well as women today, what *God's ideal woman* was like and how she lived out His plan for her life—to enjoy an *abundant life* as an *empowered* woman.

My study of Proverbs 31 made clear to me that this woman was appreciated for her spiritual virtues, which pleased God and blessed her husband and children. And she was equally appreciated for her intelligence, abilities and competence not only to carry out practical everyday duties but also, to make important major decisions, which benefited her husband and their family. Although submissive to her own husband, she was not intimidated by him. And, her husband was not threatened by her intelligence and capabilities. But why would he be?

This woman had no ulterior motives in being intelligent and accomplished and doing what she was capable of doing to be a good "helpmate" to her husband. That is, she was not the kind of woman who had to prove she was smarter than, or as smart as, her husband. She did not do all she did to "one up" him. She blessed her husband and children by being a woman whose entire life was influenced by her intimate relationship with her God. That is good reason for why God emphasized her value: *'She is more precious than jewels; her value is far above rubies or pearls'* — to the man who is lucky enough to make her his wife.

I found that knowing about this Proverbs 31 woman settled the issue for me, about what a true spiritual woman is like; but at the same time, raised questions in my mind: Why would anyone sell women short? Why don't clergy or other Bible teachers call attention to these Scriptures more often to encourage today's women? Why do they not emphasize the value and honor God places on women? And why do they not teach these Scriptures to husbands also — to encourage them to value and honor their wives and endeavor to live that example before their children, so they will learn to honor their mother? What a concept. What a force for keeping marriage and family strong. What a deterrent to divorce that concept would be. What a valuable parenting example to show sons and daughters not only to have self-respect but also, to learn how their spouse should respect and treat them and how they should respect and treat their spouse.

When it comes to women, again, mostly we hear about how "women are to be submissive to their own husbands." That's right. I believe that too. And I believe her caring and loving attentions should be for her husband only — no other man. I also believe that when a husband and wife cannot agree about a decision to be made and find they are at an impasse, the wife can confidently submit to her husband and defer to him to make the final decision. But there's so much more about women to be taught from the Scriptures, which would be beneficial to them to know about themselves and beneficial to their husbands and children to know about them; including the fact, that being *'submissive to their husbands'*, does not mean they are *second-class citizens*. Besides, Scripture makes clear what proper "submission" is for all believers, including believing married couples: "Submitting yourselves one to another in the fear of God" (Eph. 5: 21).

Considering the Proverbs 31 woman as God's *ideal* example for all women, brings me to the next question: How could clergy or any student of the Bible interpret Scriptures regarding a wife's "submission" to her own husband to indicate that her *submission* would in any way limit her from serving God in whatever work to which He has called her and given her the ability to perform? Yes, we know Scripture reveals that husbands are the "spiritual covering" for their wives—a protection for her designed by God—and something for which those of us who are wives should be grateful. But Proverbs 31, makes clear that "her covering" was never meant to *smoother* her or to *limit* her from being all that God created her to be; and to be led by her God not only to be a helpmate to her husband but also, to fulfill all He planned for her. Whether married or single, she should not be limited from serving God or doing whatever He planned for her life.

Having read in the Old Testament God's glowing description of the Proverbs 31 woman's private life, you can see that as a woman influenced by Him, her life lacked nothing. That *spiritual component* to this women's life is what gave her not only a sense of balance but also, it helped her to reach her full potential—making her an interesting, well-rounded woman. But my studies of other women in the Bible were just as impressive. Women such as, Deborah, who was living up to her full potential as a judge and military advisor, (Judges 4:10); and Esther, a Jewish orphan who was elevated by God to her full potential to become Queen, and as such, she risked sacrificing her life to save her people. I could go on and on. Other women whose stories are recorded in both the old and new testaments are just as inspiring because they, too, had been totally committed to God. They, too, were *empowered* by Him and rose to their full potential and He used them in equally dramatic ways. No woman could be more blessed by God among women than the young virgin, Mary, who carried our Lord—and *her* Lord—in her womb and birthed Him to the world to fulfill God's plan to bring salvation to mankind. And who can forget Mary Magdalene who was the *first* to see Jesus after His resurrection—and the *first* He directed or *called* to "go and tell" the good news.

There was nothing supernatural about any of those women. Each one was very real, living a normal life, with her feet planted squarely on planet earth. But because of her faith in God, He was the supernatural force in her life that caused her to be *empowered* and enabled by the power of the Holy Spirit to be and do all that she did.

This was a fascinating study for me and I encourage you to dig into the Scriptures for yourself. It makes clear that each one of us women is, inherently, valued by God. Because He created us, He knows our full potential better than we know it ourselves, and He also has a special plan for each of *our* lives. We can trust the authority of God's Word on that: "For I know the plans I have for you," says the Lord. "They are plans for good and not for disaster, to give you a future and a hope" (Jer. 29:11, NLT).

With my added new insight into the woman of Proverbs 31, I prayed God would help me develop that woman's attributes. I knew I had a long way to go, but I aspired to become that kind of woman, wife and mother. I knew I might never meet her perfection, but I believed God wanted something equally right for me. With His help, I wanted to give it my best shot. However, in desiring to emulate the Proverbs 31 woman, I understood that the details of her life were definitely different from mine. But, I knew the principles were timeless. So at age thirty, I set out on my own to learn everything I could in the Bible about how I could become the woman God created me to be. Naively, I did not realize at the time, that meeting my goal would be a life-long learning curve.

In the next chapter you will meet several other *empowered* biblical characters, including another fascinating woman of God.

Chapter Five

MEET OTHER EMPOWERED BIBLICAL CHARACTERS

As stated in the opening of Chapter Two, the meaning of the word, "Empowered" according to Webster's Dictionary is: "1.) To give official authority or legal power to; and 2.) to enable."

Putting it simply, *empowered* in the biblical sense refers to someone who has made a commitment to follow Jesus Christ— someone who has been given the authority to pray in Jesus' name and given the Holy Spirit to be *empowered* and *enabled* to do what he or she could not do in the natural. I can tell you with absolute certainty that the biblical characters you will meet in this chapter were *empowered*. Their featured stories will *show* you the evidence of the Bible truth shared thus far. Each one's experience with Christ was unique to his or her life condition and circumstances; and it came at an unexpected moment in time, which had been perfectly orchestrated by the Holy Spirit.

MEET THE THIEF ON THE CROSS:

In the case of our first biblical character, the thief on the cross, his salvation experience came in the last hour of life, possibly with the last breaths taken. Let's look more closely into the scene Luke describes for us in his Gospel. It is the crucifixion of Jesus. There are also two thieves being put to death. One recognizes Jesus for Who

He is, and simply asks: "Lord, remember me when You come into Your Kingdom."

It's probable that he did not understand that Jesus was being crucified and shedding His blood for the forgiveness of *his* sins and to give *him* eternal life. But no doubt he had heard about the charges against Jesus and did recognize that unlike himself, a criminal, who deserved punishment, Christ was innocent. We can be certain that the thief did not know then what we know now. That is, that Jesus was on that cross by *choice*—sacrificing His life's blood so that this guilty thief and every person who will ever believe He is the Son of God, the Messiah, the Savior sent by the Father, will have eternal life. We are reminded of the Scripture when Jesus said, "I lay down My life, that I might take it again. No man takes it from Me, but I lay it down of Myself. I have power to lay it down, and I have power to take it again" (John 10:17-18, NKJV).

Nonetheless, Jesus saw into the sincere heart of that thief and knew that he recognized and believed He was the Messiah. Jesus' response was immediate: "And He answered him, Truly I tell you, today you shall be with Me in Paradise" (Luke 23:42-43).

That same day. That was it. He had received *new life,* was assured of eternal life and was on his way to Paradise. Pretty amazing!

That answer from Jesus can certainly challenge any dogmatic evangelistic method that some Christians adamantly believe is required before one can be saved or born again of the Spirit. It seems obvious that the thief on the cross did not follow any particular formula to qualify him to receive salvation, eternal life, and to go to Paradise that precise day. He did not say any form of the traditional "sinner's prayer." He was not immersed in water baptism. He did not have to follow any dogma to prepare to be accepted by Jesus and welcomed into Paradise. He did not have to do anything but only be persuaded in his own heart to believe Jesus Christ was Lord, The Messiah, the true and ever-Living God.

What took place between that thief and Jesus while they hung dying on their crosses is an example of God meeting us right where we are. It was the condition of his heart that Jesus looked into, and knew. We can see that believing with the heart is everything. Scripture tells us, "Man looks on the outward appearance, but the Lord looks on the heart." (I Sam. 16:7) Clearly, that thief on the cross had a simple, yet, remarkable conversion. It was unique to him and his life condition; more importantly, the only requirement was the sincere faith Christ saw in his heart.

MEET NICODEMUS:

Now we will take a close look at Nicodemus, a Pharisee, a religious scholar, learned in the Old Testament Scriptures, and an influential leader among the religious Jews. John writes in his Gospel about the first encounter Nicodemus had with Jesus Christ. We learn that Nicodemus set out in the dark of night to find Jesus. Why this clandestine meeting under the cover of darkness? Could it be that Nicodemus had reasons for not wanting to approach Jesus in broad daylight? Was it because he was a respected member of the Sanhedrin and he didn't want to be seen by any of his religious associates or friends who were critics of Jesus? Did he lack courage or did he fear for his godly reputation and his high position in the Synagogue? Scripture doesn't give us those answers. But we know humanity is the same in every generation. People are people—and self-protective by nature. Today, some Christians might avoid associating with or even being seen with certain people whose religious persuasion or church affiliation differs from their own; nor would some desire to accept an invitation to visit a church of a different denomination— even though it is Christian and Bible-believing.

Nonetheless, when Nicodemus approached Jesus, he called Him, "Rabbi," acknowledging, "We all know that God sent you to teach us. Your miraculous signs are evidence that God is with you."

"Jesus replied, "I tell you the truth, unless you are born again, you cannot see the Kingdom of God."

"What do you mean?" exclaimed Nicodemus. "How can an old man go back into his mother's womb and be born again?"

Jesus replied, I assure you, no one can enter the Kingdom of God without being born of water and the Spirit. Humans can reproduce only human life, but the Holy Spirit gives birth to spiritual life. So don't be surprised when I say, 'You must be born again'." (See John 3:1-7, NLT and other Protestant versions as well as Catholic and Greek versions.)

It did not matter how much Nicodemus already knew *about* God from the written sacred scrolls of the law, the Old Testament Scriptures. Plain and simple, Jesus let him know that he must go beyond his religious traditions if he wanted a true relationship with God and wanted to *see* and *enter into* the kingdom of God. In order to do that, the bottom line was "You must be born again."

I would like to interject here that down through the centuries there have been non-Christian people who espouse religions, which *do not* recognize Jesus Christ as the Only Begotten Son of God, the Messiah, the Lord and Savior. However, they *do* affirm Jesus to be a "Prophet of God" or a "Rabbi," meaning "Teacher"—just as we know Nicodemus believed Jesus to be, when he addressed Him as "Rabbi." But according to the Scriptures, it was not good enough for Nicodemus to only believe that Jesus Christ was a *Rabbi* sent by God—nor is it good enough for any religious person today. Nicodemus *had* to recognize Jesus for *Who* He was: The Only Begotten Son of God, The Christ, The Messiah, The Anointed One, The Savior of the World sent by the Father—God come in the flesh. He, as we all must today, had to believe in his heart and confess with his mouth that Jesus is Lord.

Some of us might be wondering if Nicodemus did, indeed, become *born again*. Scripture doesn't specifically answer that question. But it does seem to imply that he did in the Gospel of John 19, as it tells us "Nicodemus brought a mixture of Myrrh and aloes to prepare Jesus' body for burial." Further, he, along with Joseph of Arimathea, also part of the Sanhedrin, "took Jesus' body and wrapped it in linen cloth along with the spices, according to Jewish custom, and laid Him in a garden tomb." That certainly shows us the love and devotion both Nicodemus and Joseph had for Jesus. (See John 19:39-42, NLT.)

MEET SIMON PETER:

If we take a close look at the life and times of the man, Simon Peter, we see that he was a colorful character whose spiritual transformation is fascinating. We will learn about him before and after he was called to *the promise of new life* and his role as a disciple.

The Bible does not give us full details about what Peter was like at the time he received his divine call, but we do know he was a fisherman—however, not just for sport, but his livelihood was the fishing industry. That fact tells us a lot. We know Peter had to have been physically strong. It takes muscle to heave heavy nets with catches of fish into a boat. Who knows, Peter might have been one of those tough guys on the wharf at the Sea of Galilee with whom no one would have wanted to tangle or challenge in any way. Perhaps some people might have described him in today's vernacular as a real "man's man"—even though, possibly, a bit coarse and rough around the edges.

What we do know from Scripture is that Peter and his brother, Andrew, were in their fishing boat out to sea, doing what they did every ordinary work day—lowering their nets in the hope of a big haul. I think it's safe to assume, Peter had no idea that day would prove to be unlike any other day in his life; as it would be the day his life condition, circumstances, direction, and purpose would be changed forever. It would be the day to mark his future, his destiny.

Scripture tells us that on *that* particular day "Jesus was walking by the Sea of Galilee and saw Simon, called Peter, and his brother Andrew, casting a net into the sea." Since their boat was, no doubt, far from the shoreline, Jesus probably had to shout out to them, "Follow me, and I will make you fishers of men. And they straightway left their nets, and followed him" (See Matt. 4: 8-20.)

That's it? They heard, "Follow Me" and instantly dropped everything to follow this man? In the natural, it seems absolutely incredible to me that Peter, just as his brother, instantly stopped what he was doing and *left his nets* to follow Jesus. Do we realize that meant Peter also instantly left his livelihood—his life as he had known it for probably all of his adult years?

Some Bible teachers think that was Peter's first encounter with Jesus. But if we search deeper, we'll see that Scripture tells us that Peter's brother Andrew had previously followed John the Baptist's ministry. After hearing John's testimony about the coming Messiah and Savior, Andrew went to find his brother, Simon, and said to him, "We have found the Messiah, (which is translated, the Christ). And he brought him to Jesus. Now when Jesus looked at him, He said,

"You are Simon, son of Jonah. You shall be called Cephas, which is translated, A stone." (See John 1:40-42, NKJV.)

Peter must have wondered what on earth Jesus meant by that. But we know that the All Knowing Jesus was speaking prophetically of Peter's future role in the Church. Even before that brief meeting, Jesus knew the end from the beginning of Peter's life—and his destiny. I am reminded from personal experience, that it's not unusual for a few simple words from the Almighty to totally change a believer's heart and chosen direction in life.

Peter *'straightway'* leaving his nets to follow Jesus was such an astounding decision for Peter to make so quickly, that my mind races in wonder. Did Peter even have time to talk it over with his wife? Yes, Peter was married. (See Matt. 8:14-15.) After all, this affected her life, too, since he would be away from home a lot to follow Jesus.

Peter's sudden action to follow Jesus provokes more thoughts. I like to think that even before Andrew told Peter about Jesus and he personally met Him, Peter must have already heard some positive things about Jesus.

The news about Him might have spread to the area around the Sea of Galilee, so that Peter had heard all about it not only from his brother but also, from some of those Galileans. That might be the answer to why he was able to make an instant decision to *'straightway'* leave his nets—and his secular occupation—to follow Jesus.

I have been in Israel and have actually been boating on the Sea of Galilee where Peter had labored as a fisherman. Galilee is quite a journey from Jerusalem, which at that time was the hub of spiritual worship, social events, news and gossip—shorter by vehicle today than on foot or by camel or donkey in Peter's day—but not so far that the news could not reach the area. Peter also may have heard years before about twelve-year-old Jesus, Mary and Joseph's boy, who was, unintentionally, left behind in Jerusalem, and after three days was finally found, safe and sound, still there in the Temple, still sitting with the teachers and discussing the Old Testament Scriptures. That was unusual—and rather audacious for a young boy. Who knows? Maybe people talked about the incident and the story got around so that Peter had heard it, too.

We do not know if Peter made the journey to Jerusalem every Sabbath to attend services in the Synagogue. But if not, maybe Peter had heard about what happened there, when the now thirty-year-old man, Jesus, stood up in the Synagogue on the Sabbath and read from the Scripture in Isaiah: "The Spirit of the Lord is upon me, because he hath anointed me to preach the gospel to the poor; he hath sent me to heal the broken hearted, to preach deliverance to the captives, and recovering of sight to the blind, to set at liberty them that are bruised. To preach the acceptable year of the Lord."

When Jesus finished reading, He sat down and said, "This day is this Scripture fulfilled in your ears" (Luke 4:17-21). His statement enraged the religious. "And all they in the synagogue when they heard these things were filled with wrath, and rose up, and thrust him out of the city, and led him unto the brow of the hill whereon their city was built, that they might cast him down headlong" (Vs. 28-29).

Can you imagine? Jesus, the Lord of Glory, being thrown out of the Synagogue and out of the city by His own Jewish people, who also actually tried to push him off the hill or cliff to get rid of Him for good.

But we know nothing can stop "The Word"—Jesus. Scripture tells us that no matter how forceful their grip on Jesus 'to cast Him down headlong,' He just slipped right out of their grasp and walked away from that angry bunch of *wrath-filled* religious people of the Synagogue. These were the ones, who supposedly knew God and His ways: "But he, passing through the midst of them went his way down to Capernaum, a city of Galilee, and taught them on the Sabbath days. And they were astonished at his doctrine: for his word was with power" (Luke 4:28-32).

Preaching in the city of Capernaum now put Jesus in geographical proximity to Peter's corner of the world. As outrageously cruel and shockingly hateful as this attack upon Jesus was by the religious Jews, no doubt news of it had spread like wild fire city to city, person to person, and reached Peter's town and the whole area of Galilee. Therefore, Peter most likely heard from the locals all about it as well as hearing about Jesus' powerful preaching.

We cannot be certain that Peter heard all of these extraordinary stories about Jesus. Nonetheless, he was, indeed, willing to '*straightway*' drop his nets to follow Him. We must see that, without doubt, what he *did* hear and the brief encounters he *did* have with Jesus, were life changing "divine appointments" for Peter.

What we can be certain about is that Peter went from a "fisherman" to a "disciple." We can trust that while traveling with Jesus and being mentored by the Master in the disciplines of His doctrine, Peter was, indeed, changing. We may not know all the details about Peter's transformation, but we can trust that he was learning the *ways* of God, while also seeing the powerful manifestations of Jesus' teachings. With his own eyes he witnessed miracles done by Jesus. It is hard to believe that anyone could be in the presence of Jesus and see the miracles done by the power of God, and not be dramatically changed for the better.

We know from Scripture that Peter had a strong personality. Nonetheless, I believe it is likely that under the tutelage of Jesus, his mannerisms, speech and tone of voice had softened. We trust that if he did have some *rough edges*, they had been smoothed away by the teachings of "love" he heard from Jesus, and he had grown strong in faith.

Peter's strong faith was confirmed by his fellow-disciple, Matthew, who wrote in his Gospel about the time all of the disciples were gathered around Jesus, who asked a most serious and important question: "Whom say ye that I am?" Peter is the one among them who immediately spoke up: "Thou art the Christ, the Son of the Living God. And Jesus answered and said unto him, "Blessed art thou, Simon Barjona; for flesh and blood hath not revealed it unto thee, but My Father which is in heaven. And I also say to you that you are Peter, and on this rock I will build My church, and the gates of Hell shall not prevail against it" (Matt.16:15-18).

This is amazing. Peter had received a revelation of the deity of Jesus that only could have come from God the Father, Himself. We recognize that there was no hesitation, no doubt in Peter's mind who Jesus was. He knew He was, indeed, The Messiah, The Christ or The Anointed One sent by God. Peter perfectly understood all that it meant to really know the Living God, to be a true follower of Jesus. Obviously, Peter had no reservations about his faith. He knew he whole-heartedly believed in and loved Jesus, and at that point in his life, he was certain he would be faithful to his Lord forever. Indeed, God knew the end from the beginning of Peter's life. Fascinating scriptural details go on to tell us of the testing of his faith; and how after the resurrection of Jesus, he moved into his divine destiny as "The Apostle to The Church."

MEET SAUL OF TARSUS (PAUL):

We will now take a close look at the first encounter Saul of Tarsus had with Jesus Christ where he received *the promise of new life* to be born again of the Spirit. On that particular day, Saul was traveling by horseback on the road to Damascus with his entourage. He was on his way to persecute more Christians he believed to be heretics, with full confidence that he was serving God. Unbeknown to Saul, he was about to encounter the powerful presence of the ever-living Jesus Christ.

Suddenly, Jesus revealed Himself in a bright light, blinding Saul's eyes and causing his horse to throw him to the ground.

Saul heard a voice: "Saul! Saul! Why are you persecuting Me?"

Imagine with me that Saul is more than stunned. He's on his horse one moment, certain of where he's going and what his mission is... the next moment, a surge of blazing light... it spooks his horse... now he's on the ground—and blind. The shock of it all must have left Saul dazed, confused and confounded. Still disorientated but also mystified, Saul composed himself enough to think through the confusion to try to comprehend the powerful light force, the powerful voice, the powerful presence around him—wondering what exactly was happening and who had done this to him?

Humbled now, he asks, "Who art thou, Sir?"

The voice replied, "I am Jesus, the One you are persecuting. It is dangerous and it will turn out badly for you to keep kicking against the good.

"The men with him were speechless, hearing a voice, too, but seeing no one.

"Trembling and astonished, Saul pleaded, "Lord, what would you have me to do?"

Jesus then gave Saul specific instructions: "Go into the city, to the house of Judas *(not Iscariot)* and you will be told what you must do.

"His companions led him by the hand into Damascus. He was three days without food or water."

In the meantime, the Lord spoke in a vision to one of His faithful followers, named Ananias of Damascus, and told him: "Go to the street called Straight and inquire in the house of Judas for one called Saul of Tarsus." This direction from God gave Ananias great trepidation because he already knew Saul's reputation for persecuting Christians.

"But the Lord said to him, Go, for this man is a chosen instrument of Mine to bear My name before the Gentiles and kings and the descendants of Israel... So Ananias left."

Interestingly enough, although the Bible tells us that Saul was still blind, God also showed him in a "vision" that Ananias was coming to pray for him. Can you see the unadulterated faith, trust and obedience it took for these two men to face what in the natural had to be a fearful encounter for each of them, humanly speaking? Nonetheless, both men were compelled to be obedient to the powerful voice of God.

When Ananias arrived and they came together, "He laid his hands on Saul and said, Brother Saul, the Lord Jesus, Who appeared to you along the way... has sent me that you may recover your sight and be filled with the Holy Spirit. And instantly something like scales fell from Saul's eyes, and he recovered his sight. Then he arose and was baptized."

One moment in time, one single encounter with the presence of the ever-living Jesus Christ had changed Saul's heart and spirit—and his self-directed intentions to persecute the followers of Christ had come to an abrupt halt.

When I think of Saul, I think about the fact that he had a solid background in the Old Testament Scriptures, having studied under the highly respected and influential teacher, Gamaliel. And because He also knew the commandment, "Thou shall not kill," and he was a smart man, it's hard to comprehend what made him so adamant about persecuting the Christians so that he went from city to city to accomplish his goal of "religious cleansing." I do understand from Scripture that Paul spent time in the company of the Pharisees and other religious leaders, many of whom, according to the Gospels, thought Jesus was a "radical." They thought he taught an equally *radical* doctrine; and that the miracles He performed by the Will of His Heavenly Father were falsely attributed to the spirit of Beelzebub, or Satan. Recognizing their influence on Paul, we can understand why it would have been easy for him to become predisposed to the idea of *cleansing* Israel's society of all those who followed Jesus and practiced what the religious leaders falsely claimed to be "heretical doctrine."

Now, Saul knew differently. He had experienced the powerful truth of Jesus' doctrine of unconditional love for all mankind—even for His most viciously passionate enemies, like himself. Because of that one event, whatever other desires Saul previously had for his future, whatever plans or choices he had made for the rest of his life were no longer his goal, his aspiration, or his dream. His whole life had been altered—forever. Saul's first encounter, his personal experience on the road to Damascus, made him a lifelong follower of Jesus Christ and His Gospel; proving God will choose and call one who would seem to be the most unlikely among us to represent Him in the earth. God is sovereign. He can do anything for and to whomever He chooses, whenever He chooses, however He chooses, and for whatever purpose He chooses because He is the Almighty God. Nothing is impossible for God.

Paul's whole story is so powerful to read, and his born again experience is one of the greatest miracles in the Bible. For now, suffice it to say that Scripture tells us "Saul increased all the more in strength." (See Acts 9:1-22.) God miraculously turned His enemy, Saul, into His great defender of the faith. Having suffered greatly to preach the gospel of Jesus Christ, establish churches, and write two-thirds of the New Testament, Saul of Tarsus went on to fulfill God's plan for his life and his divine destiny as "The Apostle Paul."

MEET CORNELIUS:

Another interesting first encounter with Christ is that of the Italian Gentile and Roman Centurion, Cornelius. His story is recorded in Chapter 10 of the Book of Acts and proves that God knows us, sees our heart and hears our prayers, and is watching each of our lives even before we know Him.

The Bible tells us, "Now [living] at Caesarea there was a man whose name was Cornelius, a centurion (captain) of what was known as the Italian Regiment. A devout man who venerated God and treated Him with reverential obedience, as did all his household; and he gave much alms to the people and prayed continually to God. About the ninth hour (about 3:00 p.m.) of the day he saw clearly in a vision an angel of God entering and saying to him, Cornelius. And he, gazing intently at him, became frightened and said, What is it, Lord? And the angel said to him, Your prayers and your generous gifts to the poor have come up as a sacrifice to God and have been remembered by Him. And now send men to Joppa and have them call for and invite here a certain Simon whose surname is Peter." The angel told Cornelius where Peter could be found.

Meanwhile, at noon the next day, during his prayer time, Peter had a vision and he heard a voice and words which perplexed him: "He saw the sky opened and something like a great sheet lowered by the four corners, descending to the earth. It contained all kind of quadrupeds *(animals with four feet)* and wild beasts and creeping things of the earth and birds of the air. And there came a voice to him saying, Rise up, Peter, kill and eat. But Peter said, No, by no means, Lord: for I have never eaten anything that is common and unhallowed or ceremonially unclean. And the voice came to him again a second time, What God has cleansed and pronounced clean, do not you defile and profane by regarding and calling common and unhallowed or unclean." This occurred three times; then immediately the sheet was taken up to heaven.

"Now Peter was still inwardly perplexed and doubted as to what the vision which he had seen could mean, when just then behold the messengers that were sent by Cornelius were there... And while Peter was earnestly revolving the vision in his mind and meditating on it, the Holy Spirit said to him, Behold, three men are looking for you! Get up and go below and accompany them without any doubt about its legality or any discrimination or hesitation, for I have sent them." (See Acts 10:1-20, Italics added, AMP.)

Although Scripture tells us that God repeated it three times, Peter still struggled to understand. Nevertheless, we learn that Peter greeted those men Cornelius sent and invited them to spend the night.

As mentioned earlier, Scripture tells us that the Lord had seen Cornelius's sincere heart, that he had *'prayed to God always and gave alms to the poor'*. Who were the poor to whom Cornelius gave alms? No doubt, some *were* Roman Gentiles but also, they were likely Israelites, God's chosen people. The Bible promises that if we bless God's chosen people, the Jews, He will bless us. With that, God orchestrated His amazing "divine appointment" with Cornelius. He put it all in motion.

The Apostle Peter was obedient to God's instructions. The next day he went to Caesarea, into the house of this Gentile and Cornelius was ready for him. He had invited together his relatives and his intimate friends. In fact, the Bible declares: "As Peter entered his home, Cornelius fell at his feet and worshipped him. But Peter pulled him up and said, "Stand up! I'm a human being just like you!" (Acts 10:25,26, NLT).

Peter shared all he knew about Jesus and His death on the cross—and His glorious resurrection. While Peter was preaching salvation through Jesus, Cornelius and those with him believed the truth they heard and were born again. The Bible further declares: "Even as Peter was saying these things, the Holy Spirit fell upon all who were listening to the message. The Jewish believers who came with Peter were amazed that the gift of the Holy Spirit had been poured out on the Gentiles, too. For they heard them speaking in other tongues and praising God. Peter asked, "Can anyone object to their being baptized, now that they have received the Holy Spirit just as we did?" So he gave orders for them to be baptized in the name of Jesus Christ" (Acts 10:44-48, NLT).

How fortunate for the relatives and friends who had accepted Cornelius's invitation and had been present at the exact moment in time God had designed, specifically, for Cornelius; as they, too, were blessed in the overflow power of the Spirit. This whole story is powerful and sets a precedence that overruled the code of belief held by the apostles in the first Church whose ministry was to only the Jews. We clearly see that God heard and saw a God-seeking Gentile man's heart and *sovereignly* made a way for him and his relatives and friends to receive *the promise of new life* in Christ; even though, up until this time, it was totally unconventional to extend the grace of the gospel of Jesus Christ to Gentiles. Also, this particular conversion testimony of Cornelius and his household still has profound significance for all Christians today, as it was the beginning of the Gentiles being grafted into the family of God.

MEET THE WOMAN AT THE WELL:

Let us go back to the Gospel of John for our last story. It is a remarkable scene John records for us about another first encounter with Christ. This time it's the story of a woman. Many Christians know her as "the woman at the well." She lives in the city of Samaria.

Her "divine appointment" happened unexpectedly when, as Scripture tells us, Jesus and his party entered into her city on a day that, no doubt, seemed like every other day in her life. As she comes to draw water from the well, the Messiah is about to reveal Himself to her. She has no clue that she is about to have a life-changing *heart experience* with the ever-Living God. Scripture records the conversation between Jesus and the *woman at the well,* which I find fascinating:

Jesus asks, "Give me a drink."

She is hesitant, and responds by asking Jesus why He would ask her for a drink, because she knows that, normally, Jews would have had nothing to do with Samaritans. Nevertheless, she gives Jesus that drink.

Jesus answered, "If you had known and had recognized God's gift and Who this is that is saying to you, Give Me a drink, you would have asked Him and He would have given you living water."

Then Jesus said: "Go, call your husband, and come back here."

This time she immediately responds by admitting she has no husband. Jesus further reveals Himself by speaking prophetically to her: "You have spoken truly in saying, I have no husband. For you have had five husbands, and the man you are now living with is not your husband. In this you have spoken truly."

I believe at this point, she knew she had encountered more than a man.

"The woman said to Him, Sir, I see and understand that you are a prophet."

During this conversation exchange, they talked about the place where her forefathers worshipped and the place where the Jews worship, and Jesus said to her, "A time will come, however, indeed it is already here, when the true worshippers will worship the Father in spirit and in truth, for the Father is seeking just such people as these as His worshippers. God is a Spirit *(a spiritual Being)* and those who worship Him must worship Him in spirit and in truth.

"The woman said to Him, I know that Messiah is coming, He Who is called the Christ *(the Anointed One);* and when He arrives, He will tell us everything we need to know and make it clear to us.

"Jesus said to her, I Who now speak with you am He."

At that point, Scripture tells us *the woman at the well,* recognized Jesus as "The Christ." Further, "She left her water jar and went into the town, and began telling the people, 'Come, see a Man Who has told me everything that I ever did! Can this be [is not this] the Christ? Must not this be the Messiah, the Anointed One?"

She was *empowered* to witness—to tell the people of her city what had happened to her. She definitely got their attention:

"So the people left the town and set out to go to Him."

Scripture further shows us that her testimony was such a powerful influence for Christ, that: "Now numerous Samaritans believed in and trusted in Him because of what the woman said when she declared and testified...."

The people responded, "... We have heard Him ourselves personally, and we know that He truly is the Savior of the world, the Christ." (See John 4:1-42, AMP.)

May I suggest to you that this first encounter with Jesus was custom-made just for *the woman at the well.* By the leading and drawing of God the Holy Spirit, she experienced *the promise of new life* in Christ to be "born again." There was no New Testament for her to read; so surely, she did not know to call her experience, *born again.* But that didn't matter. She knew she had met the true and ever-Living God, The Messiah. Clearly, we can see she had a true *heart experience* with Jesus, and she believed in Him.

May I further suggest that if it was known that this woman had been divorced five times and was now only living with a man, she could very well have been shunned and thought unacceptable company in most Samaritan social circles. Obviously, she had spent much of her life trying to find love and acceptance—how and where she looked for it, we do not know from Scripture. Maybe she looked for love in all the wrong places where she chose all the wrong men. The world would claim she was definitely a woman "unlucky in love." The fact is that none of us knows why she had been married five times.

Interpretations of her story by some Bible teachers I have heard, have suggested that she must have been a *wanton* woman, a *fast and loose* woman. Some suggest that she didn't have a moral compass to live by. How would they have known that? I have heard Bible teachers talk about her as if they know firsthand that if one man did not please her, she simply got rid of him and married another one, until she had married and divorced a total of five men. Again, how would they have known that? In my opinion, it is irresponsible to teach about *the woman at the well,* without more respect for her and the Word of God. That might not have been her story at all.

The truth I find in her story is that although she was married five times, and she was living with a man without the benefit of marriage—which, of course, we all know the Bible makes clear is for-nication, which is a sin never condoned—Jesus, obviously, looked beyond her sin and into her heart and found her "acceptable."

Again, we must recognize and acknowledge that we do not know exactly *why* she had five different husbands. They could have died or divorced her. What is definitely known from the Bible about divorce in that day is the fact, that only men divorced their wives. The Mosaic law made clear that if a husband found, what *he* interpreted, was any *uncleanness* in his wife and she no longer pleased him; or if he had become dissatisfied with her in any way, he had only to write her a "Bill of Divorcement" (an expression or title form found in Deut. 24:1-3; Isa. 50:1; Jer. 3:8). She was then free to marry another man. The *Bill of Divorcement* was a legal form drawn up by some consti-tuted legal authority. It was deemed that such a decree must be placed in the hand of the divorced wife and she must be forced to leave the premises of her former husband. "The woman thrust out," is the term applied to a divorced woman. Just like that, she was rejected as a wife. The common phrase used in the Bible for divorce is "the sending away of a wife." We never read in Scripture "the sending away of a husband." The divorce was always from first to last, in Jewish law, the husband's act. (Deut. 22:13.) Source: Professor Israel

81

Abrahams, Cambridge, England, before "The Divorce Commission," London, November 21, 1910.

Before we vilify *the woman at the well* as some Bible teachers have, let's consider the fact that none of us—not the greatest theologian among us—know why she had been married five times, because Scripture does not tell us. In this woman's case, one or more of her husbands might have died, leaving her to deal with her grief. On the other hand, if divorced, she had rejection to deal with while trying to figure out how to take care of herself. By law, since she was free to marry another man, why wouldn't she seek another husband to care for her? In fairness to this woman, instead of finding ourselves with a mind-set to blame and disapprove of her for being a five-time loser at marriage, I think we should feel the same compassion for her as Jesus did.

Having made that point, let's really think about the basic content of the conversation between Jesus and *the woman at the well,* which we *do* know brought about her *new life* in Christ. Jesus reached out to *her.* Remember, *He* initiated the conversation. He *did* know her circumstances and He *chose* to have compassion on her.

It appeared that His goal was to help her to recognize the truth about herself and her spiritual need for forgiveness and to fulfill her basic emotional needs of the heart. He did not demean her person in any way. He did not dwell on her past or try to tell her why she had made wrong choices, nor did He give her a lecture on becoming a "holy-living" woman. Jesus didn't belabor her sin condition, He merely spoke the truth to her and let the truth "commune" with her "spirit-conscience." There was nothing more to be said. Whatever the reasons for this woman's life circumstances, she only needed to acknowledge the truth about which Jesus confronted her—and to be open and honest with Him.

When first challenged by the truth, she did not draw away, try to escape that truth or make excuses. She did not become defensive or offended. She heard with her *heart* and *spirit* and accepted Jesus' words about her and His words about Himself and Who He was. Without doubt, it was the truth that set this woman free. Her part was facing it fully—embracing it mentally, emotionally, and spiritually—and then, confessing the truth with her own mouth to Jesus.

Chapter Six

MEET THE AUTHOR
UP CLOSE AND PERSONAL

I t was an early October morning in 1966, when I came to the end of myself. I had become emotionally un-glued. I was a thirty-year-old wife and mother of three precious children between the ages of six and two-and-a-half. I had prayed and tried everything I could think of to change the extreme circumstances and the personal heart-wrenching painful emotional condition in which I had been living. We had tried professional help, and a year of therapy and medication had worked wonders. It was amazing. We had lived a normal married and family life for the next three years. But then, everything changed again. Nothing could stop my husband's regression and downward spiral. Now, we were back to square one. I felt powerless to change anything about my life. I was at my "crossroads"—desperate for an answer that would give us lasting help. In order for you to understand how I got to this point of desperation, look back with me to the beginning.

"My husband and I were married in a lovely Catholic Wedding Ceremony on a hot summer day in July 1959—a more gentle time in our nation. It was a time when love, honor, commitment, and integrity were common virtues among people. It was a time when life was simpler, when marriage and family meant everything, and when young people still believed in the American Dream. And so it was with me.

I was a twenty-three-year-old bride, full of hope for our new life together and the family we would have one day. My husband was a new convert to Catholicism, so I believed we shared a foundation of faith. After a wonderful year-and-a-half courtship and a romantic honeymoon on the ocean, our marriage began with all the happiness, dreams, and expectations of every new bride.

All of my expectations were realized, until one night only two months into our marriage, when everything I took for granted about my kind and loving new husband was shattered and our life was turned upside down. I saw the man I married instantly change right before my eyes. I heard an unprovoked verbally cruel side of him and saw scary actions before he stomped out of the house and was gone for most of the night. I had never seen or heard that harsh, nasty side of him before saying, "I do."

The next morning, he was his usual sweet, loving and caring self again, the man with whom I had fallen in love. I thought to myself, I didn't know that man I was married to last night; but this man I know. This man I love.

You might be wondering where the story went from there? Since I must make a long story short, suffice it to say, the morning after that first shocking incident, I was stunned to see and hear my same normal loving guy again. I demanded an explanation. He casually explained his outburst was due to the stress of his job. Then, he quickly promised he would never behave like that again.

I didn't understand any of it. But I rationalized that whatever the reason was for that show of bad temper in him, surely all couples need a period of adjustment to a new marriage—and further, I couldn't *throw in the towel* after only two months of marriage. Who does that? Besides, we had a year-and-a-half long collection of lovely memories together. I loved him. So I forgave him.

He kept his promise and I didn't see any more behavior like that. But the memory of that cruel "other side" of my new husband's personality haunted me. I was determined to find out what had caused such a raging, outburst. I suggested marriage counseling, but he was not for it.

Six months after our marriage, I became pregnant with our first child and we were both extremely happy about the news. Despite the fact that I was ecstatic over becoming a mother, with my first pregnancy, I had two threatened miscarriages, one from breakout bleeding and the other from Toxemia, which was caught early and I spent only five days in the hospital. Then, during our first son's birth a "surgical sponge" was left in me for several weeks before being discovered. This resulted in almost a year of battling chronic infection in my uterus and a growing cyst on my left ovary—all of which resisted a variety of antibiotics—and I ended up in emergency surgery only days before our son's first birthday. Then, at our daughter's birth, I contracted Staph infection in the hospital and was given a penicillin shot to which I had a near-fatal internal reaction, with my organs and throat swelling. Only after the second unsuccessful anti-toxin shot given me in the ER, was a well-known internist called in, who formulated a combination of anti-toxin that worked—and saved my life. After a ten-day recovery in the hospital, I was released to go home to my baby girl and toddler son.

My medical problems were compounded by my husband's periodic changeable behavior. I thought he was like a "Dr. Jeykll and Mr. Hyde." Throughout my unpredictable and rather bizarre medical complications surrounding the births of my first two children, each time, my husband would make an unsolicited declaration that he was determined to be the "good" husband and father our children and I deserved. However, he would be loving and kind to me for only a while; then, he would change and be critical and cruel to me again. His attitude toward me would be almost punishing because I was sick. Then, his whole personality would change back to his normal sweet, loving, caring self again and we would go for long stretches of time when we actually lived in peace and harmony. Did he know this was happening to him? I wasn't sure, but I didn't think so or I could not have stayed.

A changeable personality like my husband's was foreign to me. I had never heard anyone be nice and kind to a person one minute and cruel and raging at them with unprovoked anger the next minute, as he had done to me. Having been brought up during the 40s and 50s, which was a more civil time in our nation, and in a loving home where my father always treated my mother with respect, I had never heard of cruel or violent behavior in a marriage relationship. Of course, now I understand my naiveté, as I was also part of the "Ozzie and Harriett" family TV sitcom era. I saw and heard no news reports on television, saw no movies nor read any books, magazines or newspapers telling about spousal abuse or any kind of domestic violence. Therefore, I didn't know how to deal with the cards of life I had been dealt. Because I couldn't imagine my children not having their father, I went on to secretly cope the best way I knew how.

Even though my husband continued to ignore my pleas for joint marriage counseling, I sought the help of a psychiatrist myself. Finally, I had told someone the truth about my husband's duel personality and behavior. That was a good decision not only to unburden myself and lesson my overwhelming stress but also, because the doctor assured me that I was *not* the cause of my husband's bad behavior. He diagnosed me as mentally sound in every way—which gave a big boost to my previously deflated self-esteem.

This generation of women might think I should have divorced my husband after the first time he displayed unprovoked, verbally cruel behavior. But, not only did I not want to *throw in the towel* after only two months of marriage but also, I believed divorce was out of the question for me, because I was Catholic. Plus, I respected my marriage vows spoken before God. Also, I feared being ostracized by my church, my parents, siblings, and relatives. Besides, divorce was rare in the 1950s in our society. It was a time when, by and large, women stayed in their marriages no matter how oppressed they were by their husbands. If there were a divorce, it was only whispered about behind closed doors. Divorce was the "big taboo." There was "shame" unfairly assigned to a divorced woman, even if she was the innocent party. If I were to divorce, I was certain that not only I but also, my family would have to bear the shame of it. Divorce happened in Hollywood, but not in my corner of the world—and certainly not in my family.

And so I stayed; like many women stayed back then, despite their husband's verbal abuse or his addiction to alcohol, with the whole family suffering his humiliating, unfair, and irrational rantings; and some even stayed despite their husband's betrayal and philandering ways. If a woman had left her marriage back then, to where would she and her children have escaped? In those days, there were no shelters or other protective services for victims of abuse of any kind or domestic violence. The majority of women were stay-at-home moms. It would not have been financially possible for most of them to leave their husbands, to work an outside job or make a salary large enough to support their children and to provide a home for them. There were no children's day-care facilities for working mothers.

In addition, the young women of today might not realize that divorce in the 50s was not only rare but also, it was hard to obtain. There were no legal grounds, such as, "No-Fault, Dissolution, Incompatibility or Irreconcilable Differences." Legal grounds, such as adultery, for example, were stringent and had to be proven. Actually, when it came to divorce, the cards were pretty much stacked against women on several levels, back then. And again, speaking of shame? If divorced, women might as well have worn around their necks a scarlet letter "D."

With our circumstances having become more extreme with each passing year, after four years of his "Jeykll and Hyde" behavior, I gave my husband an ultimatum; stressing that we must get help or we needed to separate. He still refused. Soon after, he threatened to kill me if I tried to leave him. Terrified, that was the last straw for me.

Despite my deep respect for my Catholic faith, my marriage vows, and my fear of being ostracized by my church if I divorced, I believed divorce was my only answer. I no longer cared what my parents or anyone else thought. My only concern was for my children and myself—and making a safe, peaceful home for us.

However, right before I took that drastic step, because of "Mr. Hyde's" last threat, my husband gave in to receiving professional help. That was still important to me for not only his sake but also, for the sake of our children, as I knew he would continue to interact with them. After all, he would always be their father.

His doctor helped convince him to agree to my insistence that we separate while he received his treatment. He was diagnosed with the mental illness, "Manic Depression." Now I understood his "Jeykll and Hyde" personality. His mental problem had been compounded by alcoholism, which gave "Mr. Hyde," the cruel side of his personality, even more control. He was treated with medication and private bi-weekly therapy, which kept him stable. On his weekend visitations, I could see he was consistently the kind, loving and caring man I had married and he was now enjoying his little ones. After almost a year, his doctor was pleased with his progress and believed he was well enough to move back home.

It was right before the Christmas holidays, when we began to successfully live our "second chance" marriage. In the New Year, however, I was faced with another unpredictable trial. I became ill again, and this time it was Rheumatic Fever. Almost simultaneous to my diagnosis, I learned I had conceived again. Both my family physician and my obstetrician were concerned about the possibility of our baby being born with a physical deformity. The months of my pregnancy were filled with anxiety. But when our third child, a second son, was born in 1964, with all of his fingers and toes, we were gratefully relieved, believing he had escaped the effects of the Rheumatic Fever. It was a tremendous blessing.

We were still functioning as a normal family and enjoying real happiness for the rest of that year. Christmas passed, and family and friends gathered in our home for a party to welcome in the New Year. Life was good for the Lantz family. Actually, life was good for the next year as well, ending with a lovely Christmas and beginning with another fun New Year 1966 celebration in our new home, with relatives, friends and neighbors.

As spring arrived and the abundance of flowers around our home began to blossom, a gift left for us by its former owners, my husband began to show all too familiar signs of regression. He was a real dichotomy as personalities go. He was college educated, articulate, and by this time, the quintessential successful businessman whose life appeared to be a winning one to those on the outside looking in. But his illness does not discriminate or recognize education or professional position.

We celebrated our seventh wedding anniversary. By mid-to-late summer, once again, his private life was a far cry from his public life. No matter how hard and how much I prayed, nothing was working. Nothing could stop my husband's downward spiral. I urged him to return to his doctor for more therapy, but he refused. During those terrible months, his changeable personality kept me on edge—riding his roller coaster emotions of exuberant expressions of love for me one minute and his verbal attacks of hatred for me the next.

After not drinking alcohol for three whole years, by summer's end he had also renewed his bond with that former constant companion. And after not seeing "Mr. Hyde" during those three years, now he was back and more domineering than ever. With all of my husband's successful professional medical treatment, nothing had permanently changed him.

As if "Mr. Hyde" had not been enough to deal with; in addition, I had just been hit with the heartbreaking news that our baby boy had not escaped the effects of my bout with Rheumatic Fever, after all. Following much testing we learned from his pediatrician, that he had been born with profound nerve deafness. My husband emotionally withdrew from me as well as the kids. I was now caring for our three children, one with "special needs," without any kind of help from their father. So with the demand on my time and energy and my emotions, I was absolutely worn out and worn down.

Mothering my children was my only joy. Although my husband's maniacal behavior only targeted me—still I guarded my children's little psyches as fiercely as a mother lioness guards and protects her cubs. Actually, it was my children who kept me functioning—always keeping my emotions under control for their sakes. No doubt appearing to them and others, like I had it all together, outwardly. But inwardly, I was a wreck. Day-by-day it was becoming harder for me to keep up the façade. I was back to where I was before my husband's professional help that gave us those three wonderful normal years to, again, living in fear and deep emotional pain. I knew I was a good mother, but I felt I had not only failed miserably at marriage but also, at life.

On an early October morning in 1966, it happened. Lurking like a dark cloud over and around me was a creeping, suffocating fear that I could no longer cope. No books, no professional counseling, no learned coping skills had permanently changed my painful circumstances. I had tried them all. I was emotionally undone. I had come to the end of myself. Under that strong exterior that others saw, was a frail spirit. I felt isolated, trapped in my fear, frustration, anxiety, rejection, self-pity, anger and depression. My earnest prayers had not changed anything, either. I thought God had turned a deaf ear to my heart cries. I was overwhelmed with emotional pain and hopelessness. So deep was my pain that morning, I wanted out of my life one way or another. So deep was my hopelessness, I believed I was even forgotten by God.

Crushed, with heart-wrenching despair, I could feel panic rising within me. The next thing I knew, I was kneeling on my kitchen floor, sobbing, crying out to God more desperately than ever before, pleading, "God... *if* You're *really* here now... *please* help me!"

Instantly, a feeling of utter tranquility came over me. The feeling of desperation was gone. I felt a new peace. I felt something else, too, something I had not felt in a long time—I felt what I remembered "normal" felt like. I dared to believe that God had really heard my prayer this time; that God had somehow redeemed me from the hopelessness that had overwhelmed me just minutes before. But I had no way of knowing the unbelievable and creative lengths to which God would go to fully answer my desperate plea.

It was a rainy Tuesday afternoon, only a few days following the incident in the kitchen. It was time to pick up our older son from elementary school. I was standing on the front porch trying to balance an open umbrella while holding our younger son in one arm and pulling our daughter close to me with the other, hoping to keep them dry on the way to the car. Just before I started down the porch steps, my neighbor, Nora, came running across the street and up onto the porch. I had not seen her since the day we moved into our home eight months earlier.

"Anita, I see you taking the children to the car every afternoon. I know you're going to the school to pick up your son, but you must be waking the little ones from their afternoon naps, aren't you?"

"Yes," I answered quizzically.

"Why don't I just come over each school day at this time and sit with the children so you won't have to disturb their sleep?" I hardly knew what to say.

"Thank you, Nora," I finally responded, "but I can't allow you to obligate yourself to my schedule every day."

"I have nothing to do at this time of the day," she gently insisted. "I would like to do it. In fact, you go on now, and I'll sit with the children today. I insist." She smiled warmly.

Driving to the school, I went over the scene in my mind. I did not actually know Nora. I wondered why she wanted to do this for me.

Waiting in the car, I found myself returning to Nora's words, pondering and analyzing each one. Why would anyone want to obligate themselves to another person at a specific time every day? I decided Nora was indeed an unusual person. I remembered when first meeting her, she seemed different from most people; nice—and warm—but different. I had wondered back then what the difference was, but I could not put my finger on it. I had even mentioned it to my husband, although I could not explain why she left me with that impression.

When we arrived home, Nora and the kids met us at the door. "Hi," I said, looking down at the little ones. "Were you good for Nora?" Nora smiled at both of them and said, "Yes, indeed. They were very good. We got along just fine, didn't we, kids? And I'll be back tomorrow."

What do I say? I thought. She definitely wants to do this. And she's so nice. How can I say no?

"Please allow me to do this for you, Anita," she said, as though she had read my thoughts.

"All right, I understand, Nora," I said. If you insist," I smiled. "I *am* grateful. You're right about the kids being wakened from their naptime. Thank you. But if there's ever a day you can't come, or if it becomes difficult for you to continue, I'll understand. And if I can do anything for you, please don't hesitate to ask me. Okay?"

Nora lingered there at the front door for a moment and looked directly into my eyes. "Anita," she said softly, "Jesus loves you. He sees your burden, and He will help you with it."

Without waiting for my response, she stepped through the open door and down the porch steps. I stood there speechless, while watching Nora cross the street. I was flabbergasted! Dumbfounded! Silently, I wondered, why did she say that? What's happening to me? I want to cry.

No one I knew had ever mentioned the name Jesus to me in conversation. That was a name spoken only in church by the priest or spoken to me by my catechism teacher when I was young. Nora's words went over and over in my mind the rest of the day: 'Jesus loves you. He sees your burden, and He will help you with it'.

On the third day, Nora shared an experience that both she and her husband had one night in a little church they had been invited to attend by friends who had become new Christians. This experience, she said, changed their lives.

"After preaching the gospel message, the minister gave an altar call," she said. "Ray and I went forward, knelt at the altar, and gave our lives to Jesus Christ and we were born again. We're not the same people we were before that church service, Anita. Ray used to be an alcoholic, but that all changed too," she said, and went on to share the rest of her story. Then she declared with joy, "Oh, it's been wonderful these last few years."

My heart was pounding; my thoughts were racing: I've never heard anything like this in my life. I don't understand the meaning of "altar call" and "born again," but I believe her completely.

It was her genuineness and sincerity that caused me to believe every word. Had it been someone else— maybe someone not so kind, not so real—I might have hoped the phone would ring or the children would interrupt.

"How wonderful, Nora. God has really been good to you and Ray."

"Yes," she smiled, "and I praise Jesus every day for the new life I have—Ray too. I love Jesus with all my heart, Anita. I just never would have believed we would be in a church that night. Neither of us was ever a churchgoer. But I'm sure glad we accepted that invitation. Jesus not only changed us completely, but He's changed our future."

Oh God, this is real, I thought to myself. I'm certain of it. All my life, I've wanted to believe this is the kind of thing You do for people.

"Nora, I believe you." I said with enthusiasm and quickly added, "I've always believed in Jesus and God, and I've gone to church all my life."

A long silence filled the room. Nora gazed directly into my eyes— just as she had that first day. She firmly but lovingly asked, "Yes, Anita, I know you believe, but have you been born again?"

I was taken aback, puzzled. Silently, I wondered, what is she talking about? What does she mean by "born again?"

Being Catholic, I had absolutely no idea what Protestants believed or how they expressed their beliefs. This was no time for pride, so I asked the question: "What do you mean by born again? I've never heard that phrase used to describe a Christian."

"Anita, that's what it means to be a Christian."

"I still don't understand, Nora. Is that what your Protestant church calls being a Christian?"

She smiled and said, "No, Honey, that's what the Bible calls it. That's what Jesus said to Nicodemus in the Gospel of John, Chapter 3: 'Except a man be born again he cannot see the kingdom of God'... 'Marvel not that I said you must be born again'." After quoting those verses, she explained, "It's not Protestant or Catholic, Anita—it's Bible. It's a command from Jesus to everyone; whosoever will come to Him, believing in Him with all their heart, can be born again and enter the kingdom of God.

"Think of it like this, Anita. In the natural, we're conceived in our mother's womb, and nine months later we are born; we're alive, and we have physical life, we're born of the flesh. When we're born again, we come alive spiritually, inside. Our spirit is alive and we're born of the Spirit."

That made some sense to me, but I still did not understand how one became born again. "I'm happy for you and your husband for the experience you've had, Nora, and I'm glad you told me about it. But I must admit that it provokes a lot of questions for me."

"It's all in your Bible, Anita," she declared cheerfully and quoted another Scripture verse, which amazed me. Clearly Nora was not trying to impress me with her ability to memorize Scripture. On the contrary, she was so humble when she spoke those verses that I was deeply moved. I need to buy a Bible, I thought. Nora assumes that I have one. I can't tell her I don't own a Bible. What would she think of me? I call myself a Christian but don't even own a Bible?

When Nora left, I pondered her story and the Bible verses she had quoted. Despite her explanations, I still was not clear about her question, 'I know you believe, but have you been born again?' Have I? I asked myself. I'm thirty years old and have never heard this. I wondered how I could have lived all these years, attended Mass every Sunday, and yet could not recall having ever been taught or encouraged to become born again.

Why not? I wondered. Especially, if those words were so important that Jesus Himself spoke them—and they're in the Bible. I remembered the words Nora had quoted that Jesus spoke: 'Except a man be born again, he cannot see the kingdom of God'. I'll never forget those words. (See John 3:1-7.)

I realized right then, that no one could argue with those words Jesus spoke about how we must be 'born again'—not even the most learned Christian theologian in the world! In fact, I muttered, "Who would dare? They're Jesus' own words!"

After reasoning this, I concluded that if I did not spiritually understand what that phrase 'born again' meant, then maybe I had *not* been 'born again' as Nora had.

Although I still had lots of questions, there was a kind of peace inside me, meshed with a nervous excitement, as Nora's story played over and over in my mind. My thoughts raced: Could God change me as He did Nora? Could He change Alex? Could he take his alcohol addiction away like He did Ray's? Maybe, the gambling too? But mostly, God, I wish You could free him once and for all from his illness, that other ugly, dark side of his personality. Nora is so happy. God, I love what You did for her and her husband and family.

Thinking about Nora's story made me more conscious of God in a real way, more conscious of the reality of His actual interest and involvement in the everyday lives of people. That's what I always wondered about. But before Nora and her husband, I had never heard of God doing anything like that for any other Christian I knew. I could tell how close Nora was to Him. When she shared her story, she radiated such happiness. Her relationship with God seemed direct, as though she did not have to be in church to feel close to Him. She talked about Jesus as though He were her dearest friend. I envied her in a good way, and my silent wish was more of a prayer: I wish I knew God and the Bible like Nora does. If I did, maybe God could change me... change our lives, too. Oh God, I wish You would.

I lay in bed that night, my mind absorbed with the details of Nora's story and our conversation about Jesus and the Bible. Nora had not been a church-goer throughout her early years and the years of her marriage; but she had an experience one night that changed her life and caused her to know Jesus, her "Living Savior," as she called Him, and to know the Scriptures. I had never heard another Christian— Catholic or Protestant—speak of Jesus Christ as Nora did.

My thoughts shifted to my own relationship with God. It had been humbling to admit just how ignorant I was of God's Holy Scriptures, especially since I had attended Mass almost every Sunday of my life. Yes,

I had heard portions of the Old and New Testaments read at every Mass, the Epistles and the Gospels; but I realized there must be a whole lot in between that I have missed. Further, I was humbled by the obvious contrast between Nora and me. I felt there was a big gap between Nora's knowledge of Jesus and my own. I had questions.

Since I had been baptized as a baby, I thought I had always been a Christian. I knew I had been just as attentive in Mass as members of my family or any other Catholic; and I always believed what I was taught about God and Jesus in catechism classes. Have I taken my Christianity for granted because I was baptized and go to Mass each Sunday? Nora refers to Jesus as her "personal" Savior and that Scripture she quoted about Jesus saying, "You must be born again" disturbs me. Is it possible that without knowing Jesus' words, I have only believed intellectually?

Also, Nora knew I was Catholic, but she never indicated that she was interested in discussing the differences in church doctrines. I was impressed with that. She had not even mentioned the name of her church. She only told me about Jesus, the Christ. None of her words contradicted what I already believed, but rather, her words amplified the foundation of what I already believed about God.

The next day Nora and I talked again. She had brought her Bible with her. It looked worn from use. All my life I had never questioned anything I had learned about God. Now, I was full of questions for Nora. Listening to her answer each one with Scripture was amazing, but humbling too. Each day that week, Nora left me wanting to hear more about the Bible. I longed to know Jesus Christ in the personal, intimate way she knew Him. Nora gently introduced me to more and more of the Holy Scriptures, and I would spend the rest of the afternoon and evening reflecting on them. I had my Catholic Missal and various prayer books, but I still did not have the nerve to tell her that I did not own a Bible. However, I intended to buy one soon.

The following Monday morning, Nora invited me to her home for coffee. There she showed me a Bible her church had awarded her for perfect adult Sunday school attendance. "I have been praying that God would show me who I should give it to," she said, "and you are the one."

"Oh, how nice... thank you so much, Nora." She doesn't know I don't own a Bible, I thought. But then I realized that God knew. Nora had prayed about it, and I was sure, even though I had known her only a short time, that God answered her prayers.

After I got home, I held my gift tenderly, inspecting it carefully. Rubbing my hands over the white faux leather cover with embossed metallic gold letters, I read, "Holy Bible." I whispered, "Thank you, God." Turning it on its side, I read, "Red Letter Edition, King James Version." Opening the cover to the first page, titled in Old English lettering, I read, "Presented to," with my name, followed by Nora's name and the date. I reached for my pen and proudly wrote under Nora's name: "My Christian friend and neighbor."

My daily routine changed after she gave me that Bible. Before, I did get up early, long before my family, to have my time alone. I had created my "special place" in this house, where I spent my time reading novels and magazines or working on my sewing projects— whatever required uninterrupted time. Now I began using that time for reading my new Bible. From the first morning, I was determined to search the Gospels to learn what Jesus says about being a Christian. I prayerfully concentrated on the red words of Jesus, telling Him I wanted to know the truth about being "born again," and about being a true Christian.

I went on reading the Scriptures only to find myself absorbed, looking into the reference verses, until I had studied several chapters before the family awakened, prompting my morning routine. Amazingly, I was reading so much more about Jesus Christ than I had ever known—and much more than I had previously learned in catechism. Jesus taught exceedingly more about being a true believer and a true follower of His that I needed to learn and practice, if I were to be a born again Christian. I had an insatiable hunger for truth about God, truth about myself, truth about everything. I simply could not get enough of the Scriptures.

I read and studied and prayed for the rest of that week. All that I was learning brought amazing understanding and insight; including, knowing that I did, indeed, need to be "born again."

One particular night, the Lord revealed so much to me that it brought deep conviction and caused me to repent of my sins and then gave me the ability to forgive those who had sinned against me—especially, my husband. God had personally ministered to me. It was a remarkable night I will never forget.

The next morning, I was tempted to tell Alex some of what I had experienced, when he came to the breakfast table, but I reminded myself that I would not be able to explain all that had happened to me. There was only one person I felt I could tell. I just wanted Alex to leave the house so I could telephone Nora.

"Nora…" I said, when she came on the line. Strangely, I could not go on with what I intended to say. My voice began trembling. I began to cry.

"What's wrong, Anita?"

"I don't know what's wrong with me, Nora. I guess I need help." I could not speak anymore. All I could do was cry.

"Would you like to come to my house?" she asked gently.

"Please."

When the children and I arrived, two ladies from Nora's church were there. Nora introduced us, and then she took the kids to the playroom and I joined the other ladies. When Nora returned, without questioning me about why I was crying earlier, she quietly asked if I would like them to pray with me. I answered, "Yes, please," as Nora took my hand, gently leading me into her family room.

The four of us knelt, and they began to pray aloud one by one. I only listened. I didn't know how to pray like they did. At once, I found myself caught up with my own thoughts. The Scriptures in my new Bible that I had meditated on the previous day, and all that had happened to me the night before, came back to my mind.

I knelt there silently, in my own deep reflection. Then, I just started talking to God in my mind: God, I want to really love You... love You with my whole heart. And I want to love others too. I want to know You... really know You like Nora does. I want to be born again like her... and like Nora, I promise I will do what she does... I will tell people about You.

I was oblivious to everything except my desire for God. Then for some odd reason, a particular painting of Jesus Christ on the cross, flashed in my mind. I had seen it when I was a child: A lily-white-skinned Jesus, with a crown of thorns on His head, spikes in His hands and feet, and a spear-puncture to His side, with only thin streaks of red, representing His blood, running from those ruptures in His body. I remembered thinking that those thin red streaks reminded me of a pricked finger with a small trickle of blood running from it.

Suddenly, I saw in my mind's eye or in a vision, I do not know, Jesus hanging on the cross. I winced. He was a mass of pulverized flesh, with blood gushing from every wound, rupture, gash, rip, pierce and puncture from the top of His head to the spikes driven into His hands and feet, blood covered his entire body. It was unimaginable.

My heart was in agony. I doubled over in deep sobs, silently mourning, My Jesus. Oh, my dear Jesus... You suffered so much for me. Then, I wanted to shout, "That artist's portrayal is not true. That's not my Jesus. This is my Jesus!"

Unexpectedly, I heard myself quietly pleading aloud, "Please, please dear Jesus forgive me for living my whole life without putting You first as Your Word says I must... for not loving You with my whole heart, my whole soul, and my whole mind. I do love You now, Lord Jesus... I love You with my whole heart."

My tears stopped. I felt as though I had been lifted up with the Lord and was totally alone with Him. I believed if I had died that moment, I would have been with Jesus. Perfect peace surrounded me. I was conscious of it feeling like that same sense of calm, perfect tranquility I had felt around me in the kitchen, and while reading specific Scriptures the day before, and again, last night. I knew for certain that it was God's peace, His presence.

I no longer felt that deep, inner void I had felt all of my life. Instead, I felt fully saturated with love. I felt loved with a kind of love I had never known before or imagined I could ever feel. I felt complete and pure love for the first time in my life. It was the sense of being utterly, absolutely, unconditionally loved.

Suddenly, I was aware that the women, still kneeling, had stopped praying and were silent. I opened my eyes and saw three sweet, smiling faces gazing back at me.

We all stood up, and one by one Nora and her friends hugged me. I found myself saying to each of them, "I love you... and I love Jesus so much."

They laughed and said they loved me too.

I felt so much love inside that I wanted to run outside and shout "I love you" to the whole world. The ladies stood there just smiling at me and at one another.

"Oh Nora, I feel wonderful. I feel like an enormous weight has been lifted from me. I feel like I've just had a shower inside and I'm squeaky clean," I laughed. "I feel so much joy... I feel brand-new!"

"You are," Nora said with a smile. "You are brand-new. You've been born again!"

"I have? Yes... yes, I know I have, Nora. I really know I'm born again!"

Only moments before, the words of Jesus in the Gospel of John, 'You must be born again', were still a mystery to me. But now, like Nora, I knew that I knew that I knew, experientially, the reality of those words. I knew Jesus was alive. I knew my spirit had come alive within me; and for the first time in my life, I knew I was miraculously connected to the Living God. That day, October 30. 1966, my life changed.

I couldn't wait to get home that afternoon to tell my husband what had happened to me. When I did, he listened intently to every detail. I asked him to forgive me of anything I had ever done or said to make him unhappy over the course of our marriage. He said, "Sure, I forgive you."

I wished he had asked my forgiveness as well. But at least, he did tell me he was *very* happy for me. I was so full of faith, enthusiastically I asked if he would like us to pray together right then for him to be born again? But at that time, he wasn't interested. Wisely, I dropped the subject. It was enough for now that he respected my experience with Christ. After that, he started asking me to pray about situations related to his job, and we did begin praying together about various family and home matters.

Earnestly, I especially prayed for my husband and children to be born again. Then, I found in the Bible that as the direct result of my born again experience, our family could come to know God's promise of household salvation: "Believe on the Lord Jesus Christ, and you will be saved, and your household" (Acts: 16:31, NKJV).

After the miraculous healing power of God touched our younger son, the Lord answered my prayer for each member of my family to know Him. First, my husband's conversion took place, then one by one our children invited Jesus to live in their hearts.

With my born again experience, God set me on the path He had planned for me. Over the years, nothing has given me more joy than telling people about the unconditional love Jesus Christ has for them and the many ways He wants to bless them. I pray that God will permit me to go on serving Him in whatever way He wills, according to His Word: "Let me proclaim Your power to this new generation, Your mighty miracles to all who come after me" (Ps. 71:18b).

I am ever grateful for the Lord's many blessings on my life and that of my family. To God is and ever shall be the glory!

As you can see, my first encounter with Christ was different from Nora's or from the first encounters of those biblical characters we've looked at. It was my *unique* encounter, custom-made for me—my "divine appointment," orchestrated by God the Holy Spirit. As an *empowered Christian woman*, I would go on to receive other Bible promises God made available to me, as to all believers. I will always be grateful to God for sending my lovely neighbor and friend, Nora, to tell me about Jesus. She was the perfect example to me for how to be a witness for Christ and show His love to others. We enjoyed a faithful friendship throughout the years and our love for one another in Christ was pure, rich and full, until the day God called Nora home.

Some of my greatest blessings over the years were meeting the six *empowered* Christian women I will introduce you to in the following chapters—women whose inspiring and spiritually powerful stories I am honored to present.

Chapter Seven

MEET JOY BRIGGS

Joy was living an ideal life and had no clue that an even better, best life, an abundant life actually existed for her.

I first met Joy on August 14, 1960. We both had become mothers for the first time that day, having given birth to our beautiful, healthy baby boys. We had been assigned to share a room on the maternity ward of that local hospital. Joy was a pretty woman, articulate, easy to talk with, and she had a great sense of humor. By the end of our stay we had become friends and talked on the phone regularly. Joy had what most people would describe as an enviable happy marriage and family life. In fact, Joy thought her life was as *good* as it gets.

After I became born again, I shared my testimony with Joy and she felt prompted to begin her own search. It wasn't long before she, too, received *the promise of new life* and discovered she was now living her *best* life. Many times, Joy and I have looked back on that memorable, happy day, when we first met and we believed our meeting was God's "divine appointment." Now you will read Joy's story in her own words:

> "Unlike so many testimonies, mine doesn't start with "I came from a Christian home—always went to church." However, I was blessed with an aunt and

uncle who did go to church, who prayed together every night and shared daily devotions. In my eyes they had a peaceful, loving, fun home. My uncle wouldn't dream of missing church. When possible, I would go to church with them, and spent four to six weeks at their home every summer. They never had children, so my cousin and I were treated like royalty when we were there. They set a good example, taught me a lot and prayed for me every day.

When I was eleven years old, my dad became ill with tuberculosis. These were hard years for my family. My mother was twenty-eight years old, had an eighth grade education, and had a family to support while she furthered her education. My father died when I was thirteen. Less than a year later my mother contracted tuberculosis and couldn't work for a year, and in fact, she had to remain in bed. Now the household responsibilities rested on me. During the next three years my mother and I became close, more like friends than mother and daughter. When she was thirty-two, we both started to date, so we had that in common as well. She remarried when I was sixteen. In hindsight, this was traumatic for me. I felt alone and insecure.

At this time I didn't attend church, and didn't pray or think about God. I thought I could run my own life. Well, I made so many bad decisions, and since God's laws apply whether you know them or not, I was "reaping what I sowed" and it wasn't good. I was dating a man almost seven years older than me, and married him when I was seventeen. I subconsciously was looking for a father figure to lean on. Well, that was the biggest mistake I ever made. I found myself in an abusive marriage, and ultimately it ended in divorce after ten years of hell on earth. I was in despair and had come to the end of myself.

I started talking to God. "Why am I in this situation? What should I do? How do I know what is the right thing?" I didn't trust myself anymore. In the meantime, the nicest family moved next door to me and we became friends. I spent a lot of time with them, and found they had a peaceful, loving, fun home. They prayed together, went to church together and showed love and consideration for one another. I realized after quite a while that this was a home like my aunt's, and the only other one I knew of. I set my goals accordingly. Also, during this time they invited me to church with them, and bought me a Bible. (May I say that I have never been led to buy a Bible for anyone who did not get born again?) During this time I began praying little prayers, asking for direction.

The "direction" was northwest to Columbus, Ohio. Earlier, I had worked for IBM in Charleston, West Virginia, and my manager had moved to Columbus. I went there, contacted him and was hired immediately. The very next week I started to work and met Bill Briggs. We eventually started dating and married. Believe me, I prayed about that decision. Bill would have said we were lucky. I knew it wasn't luck, but the answer to my prayers.

After we married, we made a commitment to join hands and pray together every night. It has always been a blessing, and the Lord honored that. I realized that I now had a peaceful, loving, fun home and family, because we had made God the foundation, even though it was only a small beginning. I didn't yet know God or understand His Word, but I knew I needed His guidance and wisdom in order to have in my family what I had always longed for.

When we were five years and two children into our marriage, I gradually became interested in knowing more about the faith I belonged to. Anita, who was my closest friend at the time was Roman Catholic, her husband now a convert to Catholicism had previously been Baptist, and we were Presbyterian. One day during a phone conversation she asked me what our church believed. Wow! I was so convicted and ashamed to say I didn't know, but I'd find out and let her know. Well, did I ever have my world turned upside down!

NOW THE FUN BEGINS.

Our pastor had married us and was a personal friend whom I looked up to and respected. I asked him what our church doctrine was. He explained his own personal views, and I was shocked to learn that he didn't believe in the biblical miracles, the virgin birth, the resurrection, or any of Moses' writings. Although I was sure his biblical views were not espoused by all Presbyterian ministers, I couldn't stay in that church. I knew I couldn't trust him to teach me. I had put my faith in a man who had no faith. We started visiting other churches of several different mainline denominations, and I questioned their pastors concerning miracles, the virgin birth, and divine healing and found they didn't believe them either. I was so ignorant of the Scriptures, but still, I would stand up to those ministers and proclaim—even though I didn't know the Bible—that I believed all of it, and that I would not be in their shoes for anything!

I started my mission and search for truth. This was in the early 1960's. Soon followed the "God is dead" movement, the court decision to keep prayer out of schools, and a general trend to discredit everything

Christian in our society. More and more I realized I was responsible to teach my children. But I was still so ignorant of the Bible!

We found a church that taught the Word of God and believed all of it. We began attending regularly, and I would never miss Sunday school. One Sunday after church the teacher's wife and I were talking, when she looked me right in the eye and asked "Does Jesus live in your heart?" I thought for a moment and answered, "No, I guess if He did I'd know it, wouldn't I?" "Oh, yes!" she said, "you'd know it!" and I could see in her eyes that she did. I asked the Lord to show me what she meant.

Anita, whose question on the phone had started my search, continued on her search at the same time, and we talked often about it. She had a son who had profound nerve deafness; that is, he had been born with an impaired auditory nerve. That was grim news, and a real heartache for her and her family. They could not communicate with him, and it became increasingly difficult. I was a firsthand-observer and always there for her, with emotional support. Soon, she became born again and shared her experience with me. We started reading our Bibles and discussing what we read.

Then, she took her now five-and-a-half-year-old son, to a local church for a Kathryn Kuhlman healing service. Without anyone touching him or praying specifically for him, but just sitting in the congregation—he was instantaneously healed. And his healing was medically confirmed.

Because I had known him from birth, I was a firsthand witness to his hearing and speaking for the first time as well as the other changes in him after the Lord touched him. Here was a miracle!

BACK ON THE HOME FRONT

At this time a group of us were meeting weekly at Anita's home to pray, worship, and discuss the Scriptures. We had awesome meetings. The Holy Spirit was poured out. I started seeking the fullness of the Holy Spirit.

My favorite uncle was dying from lung cancer. Of course, I shared the miracle of my friend's son with him and my aunt. We lived in different states, but agreed to have prayer for him every day at 9:30 in the morning. On one particular morning after my prayer, I went to the kitchen to get a cup of coffee, and I started slowly weeping. I felt a strange sensation in my stomach. I looked out the window and said, "God, I don't know why I'm crying, but You do. Please show me." This continued off and on for eight days.

On the eighth day, I couldn't stand it any longer, and decided to really seek God for the answer. I had never simply opened the Bible for a word from the Lord, but after several hours I just randomly opened it and found myself at Jeremiah Chapter 3, verse 1. My eyes fell on the word, " Divorce." As I continued to read, verses 12 and 15, which said, "I will not be angry forever, only acknowledge your iniquity." The clear meaning was God saying directly to me: "It's not that I won't forgive you, it's that you keep saying you're innocent." It was like a slap across the face. I started crying. Every sin flashed before my eyes, and I was undone. I confessed them all and repented.

This was the best thing I ever did. It was April 1, 1969, the day I was born again into God's Kingdom. I made

Jesus not only my Savior, but also my Lord. I turned my life over to Him completely. I knew that day that I was saved, forgiven and would spend eternity with Him. Within two weeks, God miraculously delivered me from a strong nicotine addiction and filled me with the Holy Spirit. He took the cigarettes out of my hand and put the Bible in it. For two years previously, I had been studying the Bible and didn't understand it at all. That is, except for the first three chapters of Proverbs. They said there that if I wanted knowledge and wisdom, God Himself, by His Spirit, would teach me. That had been my prayer for years. Remember, I had long before learned I could not put my faith and trust in men.

Now as I put that promise in Proverbs together with The Gospel of John, Chapters 14-17, I was actually being taught by the Holy Spirit. I was so excited! It was just as in the last chapter of Luke, where Jesus opened His disciples' minds, so they could understand the Scriptures. They had walked with him for three years and yet had not fully understood.

Within the year, my husband and both children had been born again. The Lord has blessed me and mine abundantly. I can't begin to count the blessings and joy Jesus has brought to my family and me. He has always given us the grace we need when we needed it. He has used our home often through the years for prayer meetings and other ministry, and the peace of the Lord reigns here. So many people have come into our home and said "It's so peaceful here." Most of them never realize how that blesses me, and I whisper "Thank you, Jesus!"

How I thank Him for all He has done and continues to do. The Lord has been so faithful. Both children are Godly people with Christian homes, and their children are all saved and baptized. We all look to Him and often pray together as a family.

I've lived life without Jesus and with Him, and can testify that it is better in every way with Jesus, as Lord. As I look back over my testimony, I see how the Holy Spirit was guiding my life from the beginning, bringing everything together through the years and drawing me to Jesus. He revealed to me that when left to my own intellect and actions, I was such a failure; and so unhappy. I was lost!

Then by His grace Jesus saved me, put my feet on solid ground and became the Lord of my life. I truly am experiencing the abundant life He promised. It is such a privilege to know Jesus, to serve Him, and to share my story and some of the works He has done in my life. May Jesus Christ be glorified and lifted up by my testimony. He deserves all the glory for the good in my life. My cup runneth over*!"*

Now Joy, as an *empowered Christian woman,* was in the position to receive all of God's promises to live her *best* life. For a time, the Lord led Joy and her husband, Bill, into a successful and spiritually rewarding ministry as National Christian Book Distributors. She continued to walk the *empowered* life in Christ through the years, experiencing God's many promises, including physical healing and great favor.

Chapter Eight

MEET CARA SUCHMAN

Cara thought her life was as good as it gets and lacked nothing spiritually.

I met Cara in 1969, when she was President of the PTA for the elementary school our children attended, and I served on one of her committees. Cara had a jolly nature, with a hearty, contagious laugh. We lived in the same neighborhood, but I didn't know Cara on a personal level.

When God brought us together, we both believed it was a "divine appointment" God had orchestrated. We have prayed together for each other and for our families for these many years. We have watched one another's kids grow up into adulthood; and then, we watched their children grow up into adulthood as well. Cara and I have enjoyed a rich friendship and fellowship throughout the years. She is dear to me. Now, read Cara's story in her own words:

> "When I was first asked if I would write my testimony to be included is this book, I knew that would be a challenge because I am not a "detail" person. In fact, my husband always joked that if it were up to me the word, "gray" would not be in the dictionary because I only think in "black and white." Nevertheless, I'll do my best.

My father was a hired hand on farms in Illinois. I remember back when I was a child out on the farm, I would walk the hills around it and talk to God. I would always ask Him if I could walk and talk with Him like Enoch did. He was my favorite Old Testament hero. He pleased God and God took him up to be with Him. That was my desire. I had always said that no one was going to put me in the ground; that I was going to wait until Jesus comes.

I am the youngest of five girls and the only one who moved out-of-state. I married my high school Sweetheart in 1956. We were both nineteen. The day of our wedding, we moved from Illinois to Ohio.

My mother had told my sisters and me that we should go to the church our husbands attend. So after being raised a Methodist, I had joined my husband's Lutheran church. I got involved, teaching Sunday school and also served on the church board. We bought our first house when we were twenty-one. I gave birth to our first child, a son. We lived in that house for only four years, and I thought we needed a bigger house. We put our home up for sale and it sold before the sign went in the yard. Something like five days. So we moved into our new house. I didn't know it then, but now, I can clearly see that God was getting me in place to reveal truth to me.

My husband and I wanted more children, but we had had a problem getting pregnant. We adopted our second child, a daughter. When my son was in kindergarten, I joined the PTA.

Again, I now can see God was getting me even closer and putting me in the right place at the right time to hear Him more clearly.

I became President of the PTA and one day a room mother by the name of Anita Lantz, called me to tell me she couldn't come to the board committee meetings because she hosted a weekly women's prayer and Bible study group in her home on those days. Somehow our conversation got around to talking about the Lord. She mentioned that she had been born again and that her son had been miraculously healed in a Kathryn Kuhlman healing service, held in a local church. I was amazed, because I had attended that same healing service with my pastor and a few other members of our church. I wanted to talk more to her about that and went to her house that very day. She invited me to attend the fellowship whenever I was free to do so. I promptly changed my committee-meeting day so I could go to the next gathering.

Some of the women in PTA also were attending, and many other women who were from local Catholic Parishes and Protestant churches—and some women who did not attend any church. Jesus Christ was being lifted up at each meeting and through our corporate prayers in His name, He was bringing about remarkable answers. It was like no one particular person was leading the group. God was in charge. I loved the prayer time, quiet worship, and Bible study.

But then being the good Lutheran I was, I already knew a lot about the Bible after taking courses at Sunday school teachers' meetings and studying the Old and New Testaments for the purpose of teaching Sunday school.

The works of God happening among us in that group kept spreading by word of mouth, so new people came every week. It was always a full house and growing to overflow level. I watched women being born again, saw with my own eyes women healed and delivered from oppression. All that was happening was exciting to see, and I knew it was God. The same women I saw touched kept coming back each week and I could see that they were still loving Jesus, still healed, still delivered and growing in the knowledge of the Scriptures, but I felt like I was on the outside looking in. I knew those women had something I didn't have.

Still, being the good Lutheran I was, I sat there week after week enjoying the prayer and the works of God I was witnessing in others, but never considered that I needed something too. Since I didn't steal, cheat on my husband, have some occult problem or I hadn't robbed a bank; but rather, I had gone to church all my life, taught Sunday school and was active in church, I thought I was an "okay" Christian.

However, I remember a time prior to attending the women's group when I was at a Sunday school teachers' meeting, and I asked my Pastor, "What is missing in our church?" We were losing the young people in our congregation who had been baptized as infants and attended Sunday school and church with their parents practically every Sunday of their lives. But once they graduated from high school we hardly ever saw them again.

Then, after attending the women's group in Anita's home, I spoke with my Lutheran Pastor again. Because of all I saw with my own eyes happening weekly, I invited him to attend. And he did come to several meetings. He even invited Anita to share her testimony in one of our Sunday church services.

I believe that sometimes we have to unlearn what we think we know so we can learn what God wants us to know. What God wanted me to know is that I wasn't born again. I sat in that prayer group a whole year loving every minute of it. Still, I didn't know I wasn't born again—and no one in the group ever told me I wasn't born again, either. But I remember the day the Holy Spirit showed me the truth.

All the women in the group were praying before we left and the Lord just dropped this truth "in my basket," so to speak. The Holy Spirit—not a person— made me know that I needed to be born again. Some call it enlightenment; some call it a revelation; or some call it a "knowing." But it was an understanding and conviction that I wasn't born again. I remember coming home from the meeting and telling my husband that I knew I wasn't saved. He commented that he would be scared to death if that were he. Nonetheless, I wasn't afraid because I knew I wanted to be born again and God knew it, too, and I felt I would be.

During the next meeting, I told the ladies in the prayer group I felt convicted that I needed to be born again and, of course, they started praying for me. On April 1, 1970, I asked Jesus to take my sins away and to come into my heart. And He did. It was as though I had awakened on the inside and became conscious of God's presence for the first time in my life. I knew I was born again and, I also knew my spirit had come alive within me. I felt it.

As you can see I wasn't a fast learner. But I knew when I had "new life" and it was Jesus Christ living in me. When I started sharing about my born again experience, I was asked how I knew I was born again. I would describe my "knowing" with this example: "It was like when I became pregnant and I knew and felt something was alive inside of me that wasn't there before."

After I was born again, God did open up revelation knowledge and understanding of the Scriptures to me in a new way. The Word came alive to me as never before. I would see something in the Bible that would seem to "jump out" at me, so to speak, and I would call Anita and excitedly share it. I just couldn't get enough of God's truth. Sometimes, I would have the Bible in one hand and the vacuum cleaner in the other.

The first Scripture verse I remember coming alive to me was I John 2:27: "But the anointing which ye have received of Him abideth in you, and ye need not that any man teach you: but as the same anointing teacheth you of all things, and is truth, and is no lie, and even as it hath taught you, ye shall abide in Him." Now, although I knew as born again Christians we do look to teachers of the Bible to learn and grow in the Lord, I felt then that Jesus was telling me that the Holy Spirit would be my "Teacher"—that He wants to be every believer's "Teacher."

I realize now that it wasn't until I got into that prayer group where the anointing of God was moving, that the Holy Spirit could even enlighten me to know I needed to be born again and start to draw me to Himself. I know that now, because my spirit does recognize the anointing, but I didn't know it until I was born again.

I believe that God has a plan, a place, and a time to meet each of us, and a purpose for each of us. His plan is to get us from where we are to where He wants us to be. The steps God leads us to take move us into the places where He has His anointed people to speak His

Word into our lives. Timing is important. At least it was for me. In fact, God's timing for me was what it was all about—to move us to Anita's neighborhood and that particular school where I met her in PTA, and to be in her prayer group. God is never a day early or a day late to bring us into new life—our eternal life for which He paid a high price when He willingly was crucified for our sins. Because Jesus rose from the grave and is seated at the right hand of the Father, He sent the Holy Spirit to teach us and help us to fulfill His purpose. That's what I was born to do—to fulfill His purpose for my life.

Everything has changed for me since April 1970, when I was born again. Time moves on and so does God. When He moves I want to move with Him. He and I have walked together these many years and He has not stopped teaching me and drawing me closer to Him day-by-day. I am learning every day how to better obey the Lord and His Word. Most precious of all blessings for me is having Jesus as my best friend and learning more and more to know the fellowship of the Father, the Son, and the Holy Spirit—and my entire family is doing the same.

I'm no Enoch, whom I prayed to be like when I was a child, but I'm still here on this earth waiting for Jesus to come. I'm also still praising Him because He is a good God.

Who I am in Jesus Christ now makes all the difference in my day-to-day living to touch the lives of others and to serve them in His Name. In my retirement years, I have a "Dorcas" ministry to the shut-ins, the elderly, and the sick at our church where we now attend. I write a newsletter for them as well. Also I am a member of the local chapter of Women Aglow Fellowship International.

I am praising God for my friend, Anita, the author of this book, who stood by me, fasted and prayed for me, put up with me (smile) when I didn't catch on... and has been a very loyal friend and sister in the Lord all of these many years. I am blessed to say that Anita and I have walked on in God, each of us serving Him as He has chosen to use us.

My testimony to you, the reader, is that God is faithful; and He is patient and forgiving—always readily accepting our repentance whenever we're ready to get honest with ourselves—and with Him."

As you can see, Cara's story is uniquely different from those you've read. God is greater and His ways more vast than any assumptions we might have about how He will work in another person's life. We cannot see another's heart. Now, as an *empowered Christian woman*, God went on to bless Cara with more of His promises; and also, to serve Him in her church ministry—enabling her to do more than she imagined herself capable.

Chapter Nine

MEET JOYCE MARION

*Joyce was not looking for anything spiritual at all,
and definitely, was not expecting to find anything!*

C oincidentally, I first met Joyce in Cara's PTA committee meeting. I liked her instantly. She was genuinely nice. She and I worked on an art project for a school event and immediately, I recognized her talents were on a professional level. However, she was quite humble when hearing my compliments. Neither of us realized at the time that God was orchestrating our lives to come together for our mutual blessings—and His future plan and purpose.

Joyce and I have had a special friendship since the day we met. All these years later, we both think of our meeting as God's "divine appointment." Joyce became a sought-after public speaker, sharing her testimony in many Christian churches and before various organizations. Today, I am proud to say she is a published author of the book titled, *Grab the Holy Spirit and Run On* (2010, Xulon Press, Inc.). I know you will enjoy reading her story, written in her own words, about her unexpected, first encounter with Jesus Christ.

"The weather outside was sizzling hot that month of June 1971, when I was born again. Up to that memorable event, my husband, Berkley, and I had not chosen to make God a personal part of our lives.

Looking back, Berk was working overtime building his new beer and wine carryout business. With three children, household duties, a ceramic studio and art classes, I had my hands full, also. By now we definitely needed a break. However, a family vacation seemed impossible—impossible, that is, until his brother popped into the carryout one morning and announced that he was free to run the store if we wanted to take that needed break. We decided to drive to Virginia Beach for our getaway. (Little did we know then that it would be the most important vacation trip we would ever make.)

God had been working on both of us for some time. First, Berk was confronted by a young boy who came into the carryout almost every day, and one day he suddenly asked, "Berk, are you a Christian?" He had to admit to him that he was not. (Isn't it just like God to choose a young boy to ask such a blunt question of an adult who owns a beer and wine business?) This incident really bothered my hubby. I tried to ease his conscience by making light of it all.

Then shortly after that, I received a letter from my cousin. She had become a born again Christian and shared her experience with me. The letter was lengthy and bothered my conscience a lot. I stuffed the letter in a rarely used desk drawer, thinking if I could not see it, then the conviction of my conscience would go away. This was the first time I had felt conviction about the life I was living since the death of my dear Grandma, who was a deeply committed Christian and had talked to me about Jesus—and that had been many years ago.

Our vacation on the ocean was wonderful. The time to leave the beach regrettably came much too soon.

Berk had a desire to swing through Charleston, West Virginia, on our drive home to see his parents, so we did just that. They were happy to see us.

It so happened that their little church on the hill was in the midst of a revival and they invited us to go. We had been invited to go with them to church many other times during our fourteen-year marriage. We had declined all those times before. Of course, we always made what we thought were legitimate excuses. This invitation was no exception. We declined again. So with that, we headed across town to visit Berk's sister.

Much to our surprise, something strange happened to my husband on the way. He suddenly got an attack of overwhelming guilt. He thought we should turn back and go to church with Mom and Dad. The kids complained, but Berk assured us all that it was the right thing to do because his parents were getting older and he knew this would make them happy. I just smiled. Knowing my father-in-law usually leaves very early for church, I was confident that they would already be gone by the time we arrived back at their house. Then we would simply turn around and head back to my sister-in-law's home.

But no, that was not the way things worked out this particular evening. When we pulled into the driveway, Dad was just locking his door. Needless to say, he and Mom were surprised and I was more surprised! (I know God was the only one in this picture who knew what was happening and was not surprised.)

Sure enough, it was an "old fashioned" revival! Little did we know that the evangelist would be a former alcoholic. He had been wonderfully saved by Jesus Christ and delivered from his addiction to alcohol, and was now God's man of the hour—preaching the gospel wherever he could. His sermon was on how powerful the addiction to alcohol is, and how it ruins lives. He told how the families of the alcoholic suffer as much as the one with the addiction—not to mention the money factor that caused financial problems for the family as well.

It was a touching sermon, but certainly a convicting one especially for us, because we were in the beer and wine carryout business. I felt guilty—and uncomfortable to realize I was involved in hurting other families by selling alcohol, while we were being benefited, as this business was our livelihood.

Somehow I could feel that Berkley was convicted about it too. I had heard about these country churches, so I dreaded the altar call that was to come. Folks were likely to come over to you and invite you to go forward to pray.

But God had us exactly where He wanted us. I made up my mind I would follow Berk in whatever he decided to do. Sure enough Dad turned to ask Berk if he would like to go forward and make his decision to follow Jesus Christ. I waited for what seemed forever for his answer. I heard Berk say, "No, not at this time." I was relieved, thinking of all the changes we would have to make in our lifestyle. But it was not over yet.

Next, a young man appeared from across the Sanctuary. He pleaded with Berk to make a decision for Christ now. Low and behold, Berk moved out of the aisle—and I followed right after him. We knelt together at that altar, with Mom and Dad and others gathered around us praying. I sincerely asked God to forgive all my sins and come into my heart to live.

Berk did, too. When we got up from that altar, we both knew that we had been born again.

Huge changes came to our lifestyle as though automatic, without our trying. Before this, all our friends had been party people—some of them bought their alcoholic beverages at our carryout. But things were different now, and we were definitely "new creations" as the Bible promises.

Remember we had never been church-going people. Now that we did want to go to Church, we wondered how we would find one. Actually, we ended up looking in the "Yellow Pages" and that's exactly how we found a Nazarene Church that was fairly close to our neighborhood. And the next Sunday found us all scrubbed up and sitting in a pew there. Soon after, the pastor dropped by our house for a visit. Needless to say, we had found our church home.

As only God could do, fairly quickly He took the lead to help us get rid of the beer and wine carryout business. Another miracle. I'm convinced that our family vacation to Virginia Beach had been a plan of God, Himself; just as was our stop in Charleston to visit Berk's parents.

Isn't our God amazing and merciful the way He uses the Holy Spirit to arrange incidents, as we call them, to guide us to Jesus? What love God bestows on us hard-hearted humans. I believe, in our case, God was drawing us to Himself because of the prayers of my Grandma, my own dear mother and Berk's parents. These praying intercessors are the best thing going for those of us who are lost!

It is amazing to me still, that God had succeeded to get my husband and me to the right place at the right time.

After I was saved, I couldn't get enough of the Bible. It opened a new world to me. I loved it so much and studied it constantly. All the new things the Holy Spirit was teaching me and I was applying to my life, were changing me little by little. As I obeyed the Scriptures, I was being transformed in so many areas of my life.

Not long after I was born again, I met my friend, Anita Lantz. My son, Alan, came home from school one day and out of the blue, told me her son, Mark, had told him that his little brother, who was deaf, had been miraculously healed.

I immediately had to call her to find out more about it. After hearing the story, I was so amazed. Then I told her about my salvation experience. She invited me to attend the weekly women's prayer and Bible study in her home. Soon I would learn that was another important leading of the Holy Spirit.

When attending that first meeting, I knew the presence of God the Holy Spirit was there. Women, who had come as non-Christians, left with new life in Christ, born again of the Spirit, according to the Scriptures. Christians were receiving "The Promise of the Father"—a promise Jesus told His followers they should expect, right before He ascended into Heaven. That day, I received that precious promise. In that group of women, we were all growing in the Word of God, and it was renewing our minds and transforming us into bold witnesses for Christ.

I cannot imagine my life without Jesus from that memorable evening in June 1971, to this day. He has been my best friend. I love telling others about Jesus and His great love for them. God's plan and purpose for me was brought about by the Holy Spirit leading me to the right place, at the right time.

God opened a public ministry for me in which to serve Him. To this day, nothing gives me greater joy, than serving my Lord."

Joyce was now in the position to receive other of God's promises in the Bible to walk out her *new life* as an *empowered Christian woman*. You will learn in this author's next book the rest of Joyce's extraordinary story; including, how God miraculously opened to her the opportunity to use her artistic talent in a commissioned work that is acclaimed throughout the world. Joyce is definitely living her *best* life.

If you enjoyed reading the last three exciting testimonies as much as I enjoyed presenting them to you, then you will be equally blessed by the next three stories.

Chapter Ten

MEET ELAINE KEITH

Elaine carried emotional wounds from childhood and although a churchgoer, she was miserable, suicidal, and desperate for help.

I first met Elaine in the 1970's, at a local church where she was teaching a Bible study *for* women *about* women. She was impressive to look at, wearing a fashionable, classic style dress, with her blonde hair perfectly coiffed. But when she began sharing her heart and the Scriptures, I thought she was as beautiful inside as she was outside and a good representative of the woman of God about whom she was teaching. We were both public speakers and ministered in many of the same Christian women's meetings, but not at the same time. So we only occasionally saw one another at a church, fellowship gathering or at the Christian radio station. Nevertheless, I always thought of Elaine as a precious sister in the Lord.

Over the years, Elaine and I have enjoyed sweet fellowship, prayed for one another's needs and encouraged one another through our times of trials. It is my pleasure to tell you that among the many different public venues in which she has served God in ministry, Elaine is a former director of International Fellowships for Aglow International Ministries; and in that position, she traveled to forty nations of the world. Also, I am proud to make known to you that she has authored her first book, *Living Expectantly* (2014, Ajoyin

Publishing, Inc.). I have heard Elaine share her story several times. She always pokes fun at her Texas accent, but I know her to be articulate and a great communicator. You will thrill at Elaine's story, written in her own words, about how God drew her to Himself.

"I pray that everything I share will bring honor and glory to Jesus. First of all, I'm from Texas. So "Texas" is my first language and "English" is my second. Sometimes I think to myself, "Oh my gosh, I can't believe how I butcher the English language." But anyway, that's who I am.

I came from a very dysfunctional family and I don't say that to put my family down. God placed me in that family and home for a reason. He used all the things that happened in my life to shape me into the person I am today. To help you understand how all of this happened, I'll go back in time.

Both of my parents were uneducated. Neither one of them finished school, but they had some wonderful traits. They were hard workers. They were honest and people of their word. I look back and see how they did a lot of things right. I'm so grateful that because of their lack, they did a lot to try to make me a better person and to provide for me in a better way.

My mother, being from the south, wanted me to have good manners. That was important to her. One of the things she instilled in me over and over again was to write notes. I would get so mad at her because I had to write notes all the time. She would say, "Elaine, well-mannered girls write notes." She had me write a note for every little thing: "Thank you for the napkin; thank you for the candy; thank you for this and that." Little did I know what a discipline that would be and one day God would use my note writing as part of my ministry in a way to bless others.

My husband and I married at a young age. I was eighteen and he was twenty and still in college. He lived in a small town and I lived in a big city. His parents wanted him to finish college before marriage, but we didn't want to wait. His parents had their own business. They owned two movie theaters and the plan was that Bill was going to help his parents in the business.

When we married, we fought a lot. I was full of rage and anger. I didn't know it, because I grew up in such a chaotic background that I thought it was normal to fight, holler, scream, and do all those things. I became one of those people who threw things. You think men are the only ones who do that. I was just full of rage. When you don't know how to express what is going on inside you, you begin to rage and scream and holler. I was a very angry person but I wasn't sure why I was so angry. But Bill was laid back, very patient. Although he, too, brought a lot of his own baggage into our marriage relationship; and though he was quiet, he also was angry.

Bill's mother would often say to us, "I would give anything; I would give all the money I have if you two could be happy." That was her desire, so she sent us to a marriage counselor who charged $350.00 a visit (a significant amount of money back then).

He gave us a lot of tests. We were there many hours and this is what he came up with: 1.) We should of never been married in the first place; and 2.) We should never have but one child as I was too immature, too high strung. By this time we had three children, so which ones would we get rid of? (Smile.) So much for helping us to be happy!

In 1966, my husband left the family business and took a job, which moved us to Ohio. Looking back, I believe moving here was the best thing that could have happened to us. It was a good move in many ways. But I was very lonely as Bill traveled all the time. He had a brief affair while in Texas, so we were trying to overcome that, and I was still struggling with insecurities—but it did look like we had turned a corner and were going to work things out. Still, I couldn't find peace.

I was one unhappy person. I'd been told all my life that I was bad and I believed it. I had been told that I was exactly like my grandmother and my mother did not like my grandmother, and I believed all of this. My mother was filing for divorce when she found out she was pregnant with me. My brother was nine years old. I'd been told that I cried until I was three years old, day and night, so I'm sure I was not an easy baby to take care of. And I'd been told I was an unwanted child. I believed all of that about myself, so I lived with all this baggage of not being wanted, and being bad.

We were going to a Lutheran Church at that time. Actually, our reason for going to that particular church was because it was a social church. The people partied a lot and we were partiers at that time. I didn't know if I was a believer or not. I'd been raised in a Baptist Church; and I'd walked down the aisle when I was eleven years old to give my heart to Jesus because my girlfriend had done it the week before. I'd even been baptized in water because the pastor made me. I really didn't want to be baptized that day because I was fearful of my head being put under water—besides

I wanted to go to the Circus. So I'd always struggled with the question: "Did I really give my heart to Jesus?"

Whenever I went to a church and they had an altar call I would always wonder, well I think I'm a Christian but I'm not sure. Also, I would tell myself: I don't think I am bad enough to go to hell but I don't know if I'm good enough to go to heaven. I had this conflict in me all the time. It was the same argument going on in my head, and I was back and forth, trying to figure out the answer for myself: "I don't think I'm bad enough to go to hell but I don't think I'm good enough to go to heaven."

By 1971, I was in emotional crisis. My thoughts were that everyone in my family would be better off if I was dead—the kids would be better off and my husband would be better off. So I attempted suicide with pills— unsuccessfully, thank God. But I knew I needed help.

We had moved to another area, so we also were attending a different Lutheran Church, which was very liberal. We liked that church. I was so desperate to talk to somebody, so I made an appointment to meet with the pastor. Sometimes desperation can cause us to take risks. I told the pastor how Bill and I fought; I told him how Bill had run around; I told him of my temper; I told him how I'd tried to take my life—I told him everything! I even told him we were thinking about divorce; that Bill had even seen an attorney—but we hadn't followed through with the divorce.

This was what he said to me: "You know Elaine, I love you and I love Bill and I can't take sides. I'm sorry I can't help you." I had just poured my heart out to this pastor. I had divulged my life story to this man. Now I didn't know what to do.

We had a Bible. We never read it. But I knew enough about God to know that is where I could find something to help me. I opened it and tried to find something, but could not find anything at that time. However, unbeknown to me, God was using all of these things.

Shortly after that we were led to meet a couple from Upper Arlington Lutheran Church who had gotten involved in *Campus Crusade for Christ,* which was an evangelistic outreach. They came to our Lutheran Church to talk to us about attending a meeting to learn how to share our faith. They had "The Four Spiritual Laws" booklet and told us many people were coming to Jesus when they read it.

None of that even clicked in my brain. The terminology they were using, like "Coming to Jesus" did not register. What did register was when they told us that when people prayed the prayer in this booklet, it was changing their lives. That got my attention, because I knew I needed my life changed. I didn't know I needed Jesus, but I knew I needed my life changed.

So there I was. I looked okay on the outside. I was wearing the latest fashions and was wearing my hair in the latest style. I looked like I had my act together. And I'm with the people in my church who think I've got my act together, so I felt I couldn't allow anyone to know that I needed that *Four Spiritual Laws* booklet. I'm not a thief, but I'd made up my mind that if they laid that booklet down, I was going to take it. I was going to pray that prayer and it was going to change my life! Well, they didn't lay it down. So what was I going to do now?

Afterwards, people from our church were signing up to go to that meeting the couple told us about. It would be held the next week at a church downtown.

I got to that meeting because of a persistent friend. In fact, she was so persistent she was like sandpaper to me. God brings people to you who rub you the wrong way. (Back then we were not real good friends, but we've become very good friends through the years.) Anyhow, she was so persistent that she insisted on picking me up to take me to the meeting. I agreed, despite the fact that I thought having to pay to learn about God was hypocritical. Little did I know that God was using all of this like a "divine lasso" to draw or pull me to Himself.

At the meeting, I was impressed with the couple who were leading it. They were sharp looking. She was adorable. I mean she caught my attention because she was so cute. They had come from Chicago and I had learned that they were multi-millionaires. Even so, they were talking about Jesus like they knew Him personally. And they kept talking about Jesus in a way my circle of church people didn't talk about Jesus.

Next, her husband started talking about sin, and although I had thought about sin in my life, I had never really thought about myself being a "sinner." Talk about being spiritually blind!

I knew the Ten Commandments; I felt like I had honored my parents; I had never committed adultery (although I had thought about it but hadn't followed through with it); I didn't steal; I had never murdered anybody (I certainly thought about murdering my husband but I hadn't followed through with that, either—(smile)—so I thought I passed the test.

But then, he began talking about things I could identify with. He had us write on a piece of paper the
Bible verse I John 1:9, which tells us that "If we confess our sins, God is faithful and just to forgive us and
cleanse us from all unrighteousness." So, I wrote that
at the top of the piece of paper. Then he started calling
out different sins: "Jealousy," "Anger," and "Pride."

Every sin he called out I had never thought of as being
sin. It was like somebody had told him about me. But
I just blindly wrote them down. With writing these
sins down, I found I had so many I had to turn my
paper over and write on the back.

Now, the men and women were divided and directed
into different rooms. There were probably 200 women
in our room. So, his wife whom I described earlier
took over the meeting. She asked for someone to come
to the front, explaining that it would be for a demonstration to show us how to share our faith—then
added, "Because we are going out into the street and
evangelize!"

Next thing I heard was, "You... you back there in the
red dress." I looked around. She said, "You, the blonde
in the red dress... come up here."

So I walked to the front. There I was standing with her,
and she opened up the *Four Spiritual Laws* booklet
and said, "Just as there are physical laws in the universe, there are spiritual laws in the universe. Law #1:
God loves you and has a wonderful plan for your life."

That pierced my heart. I'd never heard that. It was like
God had shot an arrow that went right into my heart,
in the very depth of my heart. Now keep in mind, I

was forty-something at that time. I had never heard that God loved me.

I only remembered that my mother would say to me over and over, "Elaine, if you are not good, God is not going to love you." And as a sassy little thing, I'd come back with, "If God doesn't love me, then I'm not going to love God; and, I'm not going to love Jesus!"

That woman's words went over in my mind, 'God loves you and has a wonderful plan for your life'. Immediately, I thought about how I had tried to take my life.

She went on to lead us through this booklet, and when we came to the prayer, just as I was told, I prayed the prayer—and sincerely.

Then she asked, "Now how do you know that God heard your prayer?"

I answered, "Oh my gosh, I feel like a load of bricks has been taken off me!"

She replied, "Oh, no, that is not the answer. We know God heard your prayer because that's what the Word of God says, and by faith we accept it."

Even though I had not given her the answer she was looking for, I knew and felt the weight of my sin and problems lift off me; caused by just praying that prayer and meaning it.

This had been the "divine set-up" that only God would have known would work for me. You see, I could put my faith in that little prayer because that's what I believed would change my life.

I knew something big had happened within me. God is so good. After that demonstration for the group, just as the couple planned, we went out witnessing!

Bill traveled at that time and he was out of town. He came home about two days later and learned that I'd been going to these meetings. In fact, the next morning I was going to a meeting again. That night Bill came home and I asked, "Do you want to go to the meeting with me?" He agreed.

They gave us the *Four Spiritual Laws* booklet to share. And so, I went over the laws with Bill. I had not known that when he was about eleven or twelve years old, he had given his heart to the Lord at church camp. But when he went to college he had gotten totally away from God. And so, now he came back to the Lord. Now we both knew we were born again. That was the beginning of God getting us, our marriage, and our family in order.

We had been walking with the Lord a couple of months after that, and during that time we were out "saving the world"—because Jesus had saved us. But then, the Lord spoke to Bill about us going out to save the world, when our own children hadn't been saved. We started sharing the Word of God with them. Our eldest son was about fourteen and didn't want anything to do with Jesus. It took him about five years to accept Jesus. But we were able to lead our two younger children to the Lord. With that, God began turning our home around. It didn't turn around overnight. It has been a process.

I've walked with the Lord since 1971—as has my husband. Bill finally went back to school and earned a Master's Degree in Christian Counseling. We were teaching classes called, "Life Skills" but currently, we are Directors of the "Life Skills Learning Center." Because of Jesus, we've been married for over 50 years. My testimony is about what God is able to do.

We've had trials as well as blessings through the years. God has taken the hardest things in our lives and turned them into something so much better. We learned God's ways and we learned His protection through it all, as He has miraculously taken care of us.

Since we've walked with Jesus for so many years, there are a lot of things I could tell you God has done over and over again for me, my husband, and our family.

I stand in awe of the way God has used me. I think of myself as "Plain Vanilla" and I'm very aware of it, but I know what God can do when He adds His flavoring to our lives. How He can make us so unique and use us in special ways, so His flavoring pours through us to flavor other's lives. I give Jesus all the glory for what He has done in my life."

The way God worked in Elaine's life to draw her to Christ was remarkably different yet from the way He drew the other women you've met. Her first encounter with Jesus was uniquely designed for her life condition, circumstances, and what God knew was in her heart. As an *empowered Christian woman,* the Holy Spirit led her to experience more of the promises God makes available to all believers; and He led her into His wonderful plan for her life. Multitudes of people have been inspired by hearing her testimony and have benefited from her teaching ministry.

Chapter Eleven

MEET RUTH FOSTER

Ruth believed in God throughout her childhood and faithfully attended church all of her life. She was living the American Dream, but came to the place where she found herself spiritually wanting. She began her search for "something more."

I first met Ruth in the early 70s, when she interviewed me on the Christian radio program she hosted for WCVO FM, *The Christian Voice of Central Ohio,* with simulcast programming on its sister station WCVZ, Zanesville, Ohio, reaching a large listening audience.

During that first broadcast, I discerned Ruth gave God the Holy Spirit freedom to direct her. And, she gave me the freedom to allow God to direct me as well. She was willing to trust our unrehearsed, spontaneous sharing as the Spirit led. Now that is not the norm in radio broadcasting. In fact, that would be pretty risky for most hosts *and* very scary for their guests, if neither of them knew what the other was going to say live on-air, with multitudes listening.

After the broadcast, both of us acknowledged that it was a fascinating experience. We realized that what each of us shared, had dovetailed right on-message for her listeners. And equally fascinating was the fact that the last words spoken ended the interview, without either of us having been cued to wrap-up. The program had been perfectly timed. Later, Ruth shared with me that she had never experienced that with any other guest. I think we both recognized that this was God's *divine appointment* for us.

Following that first program, Ruth invited me to be her guest many times over the years for Bible teachings, sometimes a series of three or more consecutive weekly programs to cover a subject. We experienced the guidance of the Holy Spirit in the same way with each broadcast, as we presented topics related to the contemporary Christian woman. She and I developed a rich friendship and have enjoyed fellowshipping together over these many years, to this day.

Ruth is a former schoolteacher; and in my view, she is proficient in everything she does. She is a strong, but gentle and soft-spoken woman, who is utterly charming and a beautiful representative for Christ. I trust you will be touched as you read her story, written in her own words, about how God drew her into "something more" she didn't know her soul had always wanted, needed, and longed for.

> "A beautiful tapestry and coral microfilm pillow adorns a chair in our guest bedroom. It is a recent purchase, which was bought to remind me, my husband, our grown children and our almost grown grandchildren of our roots and heritage. On the pillow, written in beautiful flowing cursive lettering is, "Home Is Where Your Story Begins."

> When Anita asked me to write the story of my first encounter of "new life," I was reminded of that pillow and the rich legacy and inheritance I have experienced in my biological family, which also includes my heritage as a child of God. Scripture tells me that God knew me before I was even placed in my mother's womb as the Psalmist writes:

> "Oh yes, you shaped me first inside, then out;
>   You formed me in my mother's womb.
> I thank You, High God... You're breathtaking!
>   Body and soul, I am marvelously made!
> I worship in adoration... what a creation!

You know me inside and out,
You know every bone in my body:
You know exactly how I was made, bit-by-bit,
        how I was sculpted from nothing into something.
Like an open book, You watched me grow
        from conception to birth:
All the stages of my life were spread out before You;
        The days of my life all prepared
        before I'd even lived one day."
                    — Psalm 139:13-17 (The Message).

I was born into a Catholic family, a much-desired first child. Mother had difficulty conceiving. Years were passing. Finally, Mother decided on a surgical procedure that allowed her to have me at thirty-four years of age. She had my sister, Eileen, when she was thirty-seven years old. Today, it is not unusual for women to have babies in their 30s, 40s, and even 50s. However, in 1932, Mother was classified as an older mother.

Mother and Father loved and enjoyed us. They included us in many activities such as travel, picnics, and outings with friends, dances, and saw we were exposed to numerous opportunities as far as children's classes were concerned—and involvement in our church. One of my earliest memories was attending Monday night Novenas and other church services with Mother; snuggling up against her in the pew; basking in her warmth and love; enjoying the beauty of the building that was our church; being mesmerized by the atmosphere of candlelight; feeling at home in the comfort of that place; and being content to be with my dear mother. As early as three or four years of age I was convinced of the holiness and awe of God. His name was easily on my lips. I made my First Communion and was Confirmed in the Catholic Church.

Mother developed breast cancer when I was eight years old and my sister, Eileen, was three years younger. Because our father could not afford outside nursing assistance, Eileen and I became Mother's primary caregivers, especially, during the day when our dad had to be at work. All these years later, I can still hear clearly the ringing of the bell Mother used to summon us when she needed something. We were too young to realize how this disease would affect the future of our family. As the cancer progressed, Mother needed more and more help. Eventually, her bed was brought downstairs to the dining room so it would be more convenient and efficient to care for her needs.

One evening after we had Mother settled for the night, for some odd reason, I found myself walking from the lighted dining room into the darkened living room or parlor area and was completely awed by what I saw and experienced. As I walked through the French doors, to my amazement I saw a glowing cross that looked to be twelve inches high, sitting on the right side of the old upright piano in that room—a cross which had, tangibly, never been there before. The cross seemed to remain there for several minutes. I did not realize its significance at the time, and although it seems incredible, I felt loved and comforted as I viewed it. Of course, at the time, I did not realize Mother would die the next day.

Looking back, because of the love and comfort I had so recently experienced, I never accused God of taking Mother from us nor did I blame Him in any other way —I didn't even ask "Why?" Later, as I processed her death as only a ten-year-old child could, it was as if God was sad and He was crying right along with me. Somehow I knew there was nothing that could have been changed in the matter of her death.

After the burial, my father told my sister and me that he had to place us in an orphanage for a while, at least until he could get matters settled and under control. We were placed in Saint Vincent de Paul's Orphanage, located here in Columbus. There was not one relative who could have helped my father. He had to continue working. My grandparents on both sides of the family died before I was born. One of my mother's sisters had died at a young age also of breast cancer and the other living sister of my mother had Polio, was in braces, and had to work. My father promised he would come to see us on weekends and that he would return to take us home as soon as possible. We were at Saint Vincent de Pauls' Orphanage less than a year. My father was a man of his word. He returned to claim his children.

Dad remarried when I was fourteen years of age. My stepmother was involved in her church, which was a downtown Evangelical and Reformed Church; so, we attended her church as a family. This time period was not without its trials, but some measure of normalcy was established in our home. School was good, friends were made, school activities were attended, and honors came. My high school Principal mentored me, a scholarship to The Ohio State University was received, and a teaching position in an excellent school system was acquired.

Then came marriage, children, two years in the military, with one-and-a-half- years spent at March Air Force Base in the Strategic Air Command in California, where my husband and I were blessed with a wonderful young Chaplain and friend who was committed to the Lord. When he was in the pulpit, as we listened to him we were awestruck because we saw him take on an aura as he preached, which he did not have outside the pulpit. Talk about an anointing!

My husband, Ralph, served as a Pharmacy and Clinical Laboratory Officer. He enjoyed the challenges and opportunities that military life provided. Our baby daughter was diagnosed with Hip Dysplasia at seven months of age. She was treated at the base hospital by an orthopedic surgeon who was known throughout the country. We made friends there and had wonderful support. I met one woman, a young mother, who taught me how to love more. What a blessing!

We were involved in church and community activities. Our vista was being enlarged. We had a good family and loving in-laws.

When we returned to Columbus from the military, we became heavily involved with the care giving of family members. My only sister, Eileen, developed the same type of cancer Mother had. Eileen was only thirty-three years of age when she died. She left four little girls twelve years old and under. My parents had several surgeries where they needed transportation and care. My mother-in-law was diagnosed with Lupus. She and Pop lived with us the last seven months of her life. The care issue drained me. My light had gone out and I wanted it back.

Even with all my church involvement I did not know the reality of prayer. Instead of praying, I coped! Coping is not good enough for God as He calls us to a more excellent way. At that time I did not see or experience people praying for each other or hearing that healing is for today.

In 1960, my family began attending a downtown church and I began going to a prayer group. People in that church and the minister, Dr. Floyd Faust, were "salt" and "light" to me. They shared with me, taught me, stood by me, loved me, hurt with me and listened to me. They put "seasoning" in my life and they encouraged spiritual growth—they "lighted the way." By what they did and said, and how they reacted and prayed, they showed me something of what God, Himself, was like.

One day in prayer group I found myself crying. I cried brokenly, "I feel as if I am running away from You, Jesus, but I don't want to." I never talked about Jesus or a born again experience—it was always God—and I felt as if I had not said those words by myself, but that "Someone" had helped me say them.

I attended my first healing service where my friend, Bobbie, had a book in her hands entitled, "Jesus Is Alive," written by an Episcopal Minister, The Reverend George Stockhowe and his wife. I asked my friend if it were a good book and then asked if I might borrow the book. I brought it home and placed it on my night table, already laden and overflowing with books with spiritual content. I was extremely hungry and thirsty, spiritually.

The women in the prayer group began sharing about the Holy Spirit. I had been in church all my life, I had some experiences with God, such as seeing the "cross" as a child before my mother died, which somehow had sustained me during that period and throughout my childhood. In fact, that "cross" had never left my memory. I loved God, but still did not know the reality of Jesus or the Holy Spirit. I tried to understand what the women were saying. I knew these women—they were authentic.

My born again experience came at the same time I read the book, "Jesus Is Alive" and I knew I had received

Jesus and the Holy Spirit in my family room at four o'clock in the morning. I knew at that moment Jesus was—and is—truly alive. He was present with me, allowing me to know how much He loves me! I had told God previously that if this experience were not of Him, I did not want it. He left no doubt in my mind that it was, indeed, of Him. He chose those moments in my own home, with no one around, to demonstrate the reality of Jesus and the Holy Spirit. He moved me from darkness to light, from doubt to certainty at the faith level. And my life was changed forever.

My friend later told me that she would not have loaned that book to anyone who had not asked for it. I have come to understand that God wants us to experience and to know Him relationally. He desires for us to know Him as God the Father, as Jesus the Son, and as the Holy Spirit, our Comforter and Guide. Until we know God in all His dimensions, our knowledge is incomplete.

Oh dear readers, I have so much more I wish I could tell you. There is something wonderfully strange about experiencing God. You desire with all your heart that other people will experience God, also.

"Thank You! Everything in me says 'Thank You!'
    Angels listen as I sing my thanks.
I kneel in worship facing Your Holy Temple
    And say it again 'Thank You!'
Thank You for Your love,
    Thank You for Your faithfulness;
Most Holy is Your Name,
    Most Holy is Your Word.
The moment I called out, You stepped in;
    You made my life large with strength."
        —Psalm 138: 1-3 (The Message).

I have come to know that a prayer of gratitude or thanks is a powerful prayer. May this statement be a reminder to us all to utter prayers of thanks. No prayer is greater."

Ruth's born again experience brought her what she had been seeking in God to bless her life. Since becoming an *empowered Christian woman,* she has received other promises of God, including His healing touch. God has used her greatly, to spiritually touch the lives of multitudes of people, over the airways. In addition, she has faithfully served God in her home church.

Chapter Twelve

MEET JUDY ROSS

Judy was un-churched and living the American Nightmare when she came to a point where she was hopeless, and desperately seeking help.

On the morning of one of my weekly home prayer and Bible study meetings in 1972, I received an early phone call from a woman who introduced herself as Judy. She told me she was a new Christian and that a local minister had told her about me. She asked if she could come to my home sometime to talk with me. I told her our prayer group was meeting later in the morning and invited her to come.

When Judy arrived, we were already in prayer. She was tall, slim, attractive, and poised. Although she was an unfamiliar person to me, as the meeting went on, I felt impressed that I should know this woman better. So, after the meeting, I invited her to stay on to chat. Judy accepted and we did just that. Then I asked Judy to share with me about how she experienced becoming born again. Her testimony was thrilling to hear. Since that day, Judy and I have shared a lovely friendship that has seen us through many blessed, rejoicing times, and our ministry to one another has sustained us through the hardest trials of our lives. I trust you also will be thrilled as you read Judy's story for yourself, written in her own words.

"My three brothers and I were raised by our mother and a step-father who came into our family after our father died in an auto accident when we were four, three and two-years-old. We had what appeared to be a rather normal life growing up. I graduated from high school and after one year of college, dropped out of school to marry a man eight years my senior. We both wanted several children. It took three years to get pregnant but we finally had our first baby girl.

We had recently bought our own home and it should have been a very happy time in my life. Nevertheless, I was miserable. I was depressed and anxious all the time. I was aware of a vague pain in the core of my being. It was a deep inner sadness that I couldn't identify, but had colored everything else in my life.

I didn't like my husband very much anymore and as much as I had looked forward to having a child and was grateful for being a mother, I was also filled with frustration and it was not satisfying. I was angry all the time, but didn't know why. I hated everyone, especially myself. I felt I was ugly, stupid, and worthless. I cried for no apparent reason, and never really wanted to get out of bed.

I tried to ignore these feelings, but they were dominating more and more of my waking hours. I felt lost and confused. I had to find a better reason to live or I wanted out.

I know now that I was truly suicidal. My negative, hopeless attitude continued to affect my relationship with my husband and as we grew farther and farther apart, I took a job to get myself out of the house. After working all day at a doctor's office, I would go out with the "girls" all evening and would arrive home after my husband was asleep. Then I would sleep until he left for work the next morning. I began to look for love and relief from my pain in all the wrong places. I was growing more and more depressed and desperate. I was using alcohol to numb the unwanted feelings.

I was willing to try anything that would give me some relief. I even went to a fortuneteller and a séance where I was told I was talking to my biological father, who was my "guardian angel." That should have been comforting but somehow I knew it was phony and it left me cold. I needed to find the answers to those age-old questions: Who am I? How did I get here? Where was I going? What is my purpose? How can I be happy? Nothing I tried helped. Every attempt at finding meaning for my life left me as empty as before.

One night I was attending a ladies card club. In my desperation, I asked if anyone there went to a church that they liked. I had never tried "church" for myself and had never known anyone who went to church except out of obligation to his or her parents or spouse. I didn't know anyone who "liked" it but I thought it was worth asking. It turned out there were two ladies who both went to the same Episcopal Church. One of the ladies said, "It is really cool. We have a young couples club and we go out on Saturday nights and do fun things. The Sunday morning services are very low-key. The Priest doesn't put any pressure on anyone to believe a certain way. They accept everyone. We are going square dancing at the VFW club this Saturday night, why don't you join us?"

I had only been square dancing once in my life, but I had liked it, so I was interested. I said I would check with my husband and see if he was willing to go.

For some reason, he was willing and we went square dancing. We all drank one beer after another all evening and danced and laughed and then stole the unique beer pitchers under our coats as we left. My husband and I felt right at home with this group. The goal was then to see who could make it to church the next morning in spite of their hangover. We were among those who made it Sunday morning and it was just as they had said: the message was short and sweet, non-threatening and the overall atmosphere left plenty of room to enjoy life and still feel you were doing a good thing by going to church.

One Wednesday night I went to the Church Bible Study group. There was a married couple there who had lost a young child and the Priest was trying to answer their difficult questions about "Why?" and "Why our son?" I was interested because I too was looking for a lot of answers to "Why?" To my surprise and disappointment, this "Christian" group, including the priest, had no more answers than I did. The couple was not comforted. I began to think this was just one more dead end in my search for something meaningful in life.

We continued to attend church on and off. On one of my visits, for some reason (or Some One's reason), I picked up a Bible Tract that had been left in the vestibule of the church. When I began to read it, I felt like someone was writing about my life and me. It generally said, "Are you at the end of your rope? Does your life make no sense to you? Are you tired of going through day after day without any purpose or hope?"

I said, "Yes!" to all of the above. I was excited because at least someone was defining my condition and understanding my predicament. Then it said, "If this is you, we have the answers you've been searching for." I was beyond thrilled. Then I turned the page and continued to read, "All you have to do is give your life to Jesus Who died on the cross for the forgiveness of your sins, and you can find new life."

I wanted to scream, "You must be kidding. How could someone's death 2000 years ago make the least bit of difference in my life today?" I felt betrayed, set up to expect help and then all my hopes dashed with that foolish answer. I thought I couldn't stand it any longer, seriously believing there was no answer for me. I don't mean to sound melodramatic, but I began to entertain the idea of finding a permanent way out. I had reached rock bottom.

In spite of myself, all the next week those words I had read kept echoing through my mind: "All you have to do..." Like it was so simple. It was almost mocking. "All you have to do..." As irritating as that continuous thought was, I couldn't shake it.

The following Saturday night, I had gone out to drown my sorrows and didn't come home until Sunday morning when my husband was getting up. We got into a terrible fight and without enough thought, I grabbed my coat and slammed the door behind me and went to the car. I didn't want to ever go back but realized that I couldn't go far without my daughter or even a packed bag.

As tears of anger, shame and unhappiness began to fall, I wondered what I could do, where I could go. I didn't know anyone who could help me. It wasn't like I needed money, a job or a place to live. I needed to know how to make my life work. And I didn't know anyone who had that answer.

Then I realized it was Sunday morning, just about time for church. I couldn't sit there in my driveway any longer; so, for lack of a better place to go, I drove to the Episcopal Church, went in and took a seat in one of the pews.

It just happened to be a point in the service where everyone knelt at his or her seats to pray, to recite from the book of prayers.

However, rather than follow the prayers as written, I began to cry and talk to God from my heart, out of my intense pain: "God, if You are real and You did die for me and if 'all I have to do' is call on You, then I am calling on You now. Please help me! I am going to die if You don't do something to help me! I cannot go on this way!" I began to sob—harder and harder. But at the same time, a peace began to come over me that I had never felt before. All of a sudden, I had an inexplicable hope where there had been total despair. I had a new sense of joy that I could not describe. I felt a comforting Presence and found myself repeating, "I'm sorry. I'm so sorry for all my sins… please forgive me."

Now my tears were a combination of sorrow for all the sins I was seeing for the first time—and for the newfound joy and hope that things could and would change for the better. In those few moments, I knew that I was changed, somehow, forever. I felt lifted above the reality of where I was and the people around me. I felt enveloped with a warm, bright light and felt a sense of love that I had never felt in my life. It was as though God was right there with me. I didn't want to move from that spot.

At this point, those nearest me began to attempt to comfort me. They were patting my shoulders and saying things like, "It will be okay... don't cry... things will get better." All I could say in response was, "You don't understand. It is better. Everything really is okay. Something has happened to me. I believe Jesus just answered my prayer." Looking back, I think they were more concerned about my mental health when I said that, than when I was falling apart.

The service concluded and the priest asked me to come to his office. He asked me if I was okay and if he could help me in any way. I tried to explain the terrible fight with my husband and how I ended up here right at prayer time; and how I had asked God to help me and that something amazing had happened to me. I explained, as best I could, how I suddenly felt a warm Presence, a bright light, peace and love that I had never known before. I just knew that things were going to be different—I was going to be different! He did not understand it, but he did believe that something had happened to me. He said we would talk again soon.

In the meantime, I was anxious to get home and talk to my husband. I went in and began by apologizing to him for having been out all night the night before and for having become a terrible wife who was not doing right by him or our daughter. I told him things would be different from now on; and that I was going to do better. And I knew that was true. I asked him to give me another chance.

From that glorious Sunday on, I began to prepare meals again and take care of the house better than I ever had. I lovingly cared for our daughter and in every way tried to meet my husband's needs and make our home a nicer place to be. He was awe-struck. He did not understand what had happened to me either, but he could not deny the change in me.

The next time I met with my Priest, he was excited and related to me that he had driven to Cincinnati to meet with a man he had gone to seminary with years before. He said that previously this Priest had talked to him about an experience of being "born again." After hearing me last Sunday, he decided to see if he could find out more about it. He said that his friend had explained that when I had cried out to God, He answered me and Jesus came into my heart to live. He went on to tell me more of what his friend said: "Judy, he said that 'when this happens, your sins are forgiven and God fills you with His Spirit of love and joy and hope. That's why you felt so much better'. You were seeking God and you found Him, just like it says in Jeremiah 29:13, 'And you shall seek Me, and find Me, when you shall search for Me with all your heart'. He believes you were 'born again just as the Bible says'."

I didn't care what anyone called it. My life had changed. I was happy and I loved the Lord. I started thinking about the fact that this was all written about in the Bible. I had always said that anyone who believed in the Bible was naïve and somewhat of a fool. After all, even if this ancient writing was genuine at one time, it had been passed down through many years and had been translated from one language to another, so how could it be trusted to be accurate? But now, I decided that maybe I should read some of it for myself.

I began by reading the book of Matthew, the first book in the New Testament. I read it straight through and without thinking, said out loud, "It is absolutely true. I believe every word!" No one could have been more surprised than I was at how much I loved it.

From then on, I read it every free moment and tried to understand it all. I'll never forget the day I found

I Peter: 2:5 in my King James Bible: "... rejected of man, but chosen of God and precious." I had always felt rejected and now I rejoiced that I, too, was "chosen of God" and "precious."

It was such an amazing thing to realize that even though I had lost my earthly father at a young age, now I had a Heavenly Father that knew me and loved me—'chose' me—and thought I was 'precious'. Glory!

Needless to say, my life was changed in a permanent way. Instantaneously, God broke my pack-a-day addiction to cigarettes and I quit smoking. My emotional healing took a bit longer. Take my word for the fact that God continued to lead me a step at a time in my new walk with Him.

God gently brought forward my repressed memories of sexual abuse by my stepfather, and the shame and abandonment I felt when I told my mother and she didn't believe me. That explained a lot of the pain and deep sadness I had lived with all those years. Miraculously, over the next year or so, God dramatically delivered me from deep-rooted demonic oppression—a ministry I had never heard of and would not have known I needed, until I experienced it. With that, God lifted my shame and guilt, and led me into amazing emotional healing and freedom. It was an arduous journey, but worth every tear and struggle to eventually become a truly liberated woman, completely free of my past. I look forward to sharing more of my story with you in Anita's second book.

The Lord used some very special relationships, including the one with Anita, (which He's still using) to help me continue to grow. Since then, God has walked with me through valleys and taken me up to mountain tops as I have trusted Him one day at a time on my way to my heavenly home where I will be with Him for eternity.

By the way, it wasn't long until that Episcopal Priest and his wife and most of the congregation, came into the full experience of being born again and Spirit-filled and went on to serve God in truth and in power. Only God could have done that. Amazing!"

As an *empowered Christian woman,* Judy went on to experience more promises of God, including, emotional and physical healings. Now, she is retired from her career position and is enjoying more time for her own personal pursuits, including, more time with the Lord. She continues to be open to minister and teach in the Body of Christ, as God leads.

You saw that each woman's story demonstrated the evidence of all the Bible truth presented thus far. By choosing *the promise of new life,* not only was each one transformed but also, automatically *empowered* because through faith, Jesus Christ had entered her life. In addition, no doubt, you recognize in each story the kind of love that can come only from Christ, and the kind of power and enabling that only God can impart by His Holy Spirit.

God went on to individually establish the author and each of the other women on a solid Bible foundation. This helped each of us to grow and mature in our faith; to function as better women in every aspect of our living; to develop to our full potential; and to live peacefully and stress-free to "look our best, do our best, and be our best." Over the years, each of us has received many other promises and blessings from God; but also, He has taken us through major challenges and helped us to *thrive* in the midst of our trials to experience spiritual victory.

Each of us is still yielded to God, and still on His Potter's Wheel as a work in progress, to be molded and conformed into the woman He created us to be. After years of intimately walking with God and serving Him—some in public ministry and others in their home church ministry—each one of us has the same passion to keep learning more about God and His ways and how to better serve Him; and we each are blessed with the same vitality to continue walking-out His purpose for our lives. To this day, by the grace of God and His Holy Scriptures, each of us, continues to live as an *empowered Christian woman.*

What God did for His *empowered* biblical followers you read about, He did for this author and each of the six other women whose stories you have read, proving His Word: "I am the Lord, I change not" (Mal. 3:6); "Jesus is the same yesterday, today, and forever" (Heb. 13:8); and "God is no respecter of persons" (Acts 10:34).

Chapter Thirteen

NEW LIFE, BORN AGAIN...
IS IT FOR YOU?

Now, we will further explore the born again experience to help you decide, "Is it for you?" At this time, I especially want to encourage new Christians who might be disillusioned because of one or more of the general misconceptions about the Christian life. The following insights might be helpful to dispel at least some of the false beliefs, which can sometimes keep us from enjoying our place in the family of God.

Misconceptions About the Christian Life

•   **If I become a Christian I will have no major problems in my life.** That is not true. Even as a Christian, life is not always easy. Jesus Himself told us that in this world we would have trials and sorrows. (See John 16:33.) We will still face problems, challenges, and afflictions even while experiencing all the joys of being born again of the Spirit. We will be on the "mountaintop" at times and down in the "valley" at other times. However, even in the *valley,* Christ will be there with us. It is in the *valley* and in the midst of our problems that our faith will be tested and we will learn our most valuable spiritual life and growth lessons. So while in the *valley,* and in the throes of our most difficult trials, we need to hold steady; stay in our Bible;

keep praying and trusting; and do the next small thing God nudges us to do—while we wait for His time to deliver us out of our trial completely or to sustain us through to the other side of it. We must trust God's way, not our own way, and we will come up out of the *valley* a stronger Christian. The Word of God is true: "Many are the afflictions of the righteous. But the Lord delivers him out of them all" (Psalm 34:19, NKJV).

• **If I become a Christian I must give up all fun to follow rigid rules.** That is not true. Take it from me, the Christian life is more than fun and God does have amazing adventures for us to experience. Being a follower of Christ does not mean we must become legalistic and practice a lot of man-made rules of "dos and don'ts." Rather, as a true follower, we live by faith, the grace of the Lord Jesus Christ, and His Bible principles. We want to be continually God-conscious as we go through our day. We will not deliberately sin, but because we lack perfection, we will fail from time to time. When we do, we need only to be contrite and immediately repent for our wrongdoing in a weak moment and choose what we know is God's way according to the Bible. If we set our mind to make this a daily practice, we will continually enjoy an intimate relationship with Jesus. Our God, Who loves us unconditionally, knows how to keep us. He will give us all of His promises and His power to live our *new life*—a life very much worth living. As a Christian, if we will always choose God's way, we can expect to live the abundant, *empowered* life promised in God's Word. I personally do not know any people who experience more joy or contentment in this life than my fellow Christians do. The Word of God is true and it bears repeating: "No eye has seen, no ear has heard, no mind has conceived what God has prepared for those who love him" (I Cor. 2:9).

• **All other Christians I will meet will be loving, perfect people.** That is not true. We must be prepared to accept the imperfections and failures of those in the family of God. That way we will not become disillusioned when we do see their imperfections, because we already know the truth—that we are all imperfect and *a work in progress*. Although we endeavor to display godly behavior, we will never obtain perfection, until we stand before the Lord, free of our sinful flesh. Until then, remember if Christians were perfect there would be no need to "forgive one another" as Jesus commands of His followers. The fact is, that all of us Christians still live in a body of "flesh." Unfortunately, "saved flesh" can behave the same way as "unsaved flesh."

In a weak moment, we have all been guilty of responding to another in our own way, instead of God's way. That's not always a pretty sight. Sometimes we relate like *oil and water* and sometimes like *sandpaper* and we rub each other the wrong way. It can be painful. We need to remember that like "siblings" in our natural families, our interactions can bring disagreements or squabbles. The upside of that is, typically we still love each other in spite of it and we kiss and make up. Nonetheless, God knows how to get the kids in His family back on track again to interact His way. Because we are *siblings* in His family, we learn that He uses our imperfections and weaknesses to help one another recognize and correct our faults, in order to grow spiritually.

To live in harmony with our imperfect and not always loving *siblings* in God's family, we must adhere to the Bible and practice His ways to overcome our differences. We all need to give each other a pass, so to speak, by extending mercy, forgiveness, and love. We *can* do this because we are born again and, therefore, we have a new nature and the power of the Holy Spirit within to choose God's ways. As we alluded to earlier, when we practice God's ways, these Christ-like attributes will grow in us like fruit on a tree; making it easier for us to do the right thing—and we can do it with the right attitude, knowing we need the same from others. We will learn that our love for one another will cover a multitude of sins and overcome any relational problem among our brothers and sisters who are part of the family of God. The Word of God is true and we must obey it to the best of our ability: "Bearing with one another, if anyone has a complaint against another; even as Christ forgave you, so you also must do" (Col. 3:13, NKJV).

Negative Perceptions About Christians and The Church

In addition to the general misconceptions about the Christian life, I believe there are some negative perceptions about Christians and The Church that hold us back from wanting to get on board. I believe there is a whole group of women who, up to now, have been cautious, reticent to embrace *the promise of new life,* and skeptical about the born again experience and Christianity as a whole—and feel they have had good reason to be. But, wait a minute. I think I can help those of you who might still have a degree of skepticism, by bringing some fresh insight to these issues.

Media Portrayal

It is not surprising that today many are turned off by religion in general, and Christianity in particular. After all, secular books and other publications, movies, and television openly criticize and mock Christianity, sometimes by way of seemingly innocent TV comedy satires, which negatively portray Christians with unflattering, exaggerated characterizations. Christians who seem to be fair game for this open ridicule are usually politicians, celebrities and other public figures that disclose they are born again and Bible-believing. We need to reject this unfair *media portrayal* of Christians, and recognize that it is untrue and can keep us from knowing what is *true.*

Scandals and Rumors

Television news, although only doing its job, adds to the negative perception of Christianity by eagerly reporting the scandals involving unconscionable acts committed by Church leaders. Media exposes the moral failures of Catholic priests, Protestant ministers and others in church leadership as well as Christian evangelists and TV broadcasters. These stories are immediately carried by satellite around the globe, influencing people worldwide to believe that Christianity as a whole is failing. Of course, these shameful stories *should* be exposed. There should be a high standard of integrity in journalism and media news reporting as well as for Christian leaders. Remember, until scandals are investigated and proven true, they are only *rumors.*

In my opinion, there is an imbalance in the American television network news reporting. The media seems to televise every negative thing that can be dug up about Christians and Christianity, but we never see or hear the exposure of shameful stories about the clergy and leadership of other religious faiths. Neither do they report enough of the good things Christian leaders do all the time. For example, when great earthquakes, hurricanes, flooding and other disasters occur anywhere in the world, we always hear the national news reports about FEMA and The Red Cross going in to help. But we never hear reports such as, the fact, that Franklin Graham's ministry, *Samaritan's Purse,* and *CBN's Operation Blessing,* along with other Christian ministries and churches are also responders to these catastrophes—with volunteer teams of medical professionals giving aid and medications; individuals distributing water, food, and clothing; others doing cleanup and rebuilding; and all of them praying for victims. By the national news not reporting the positives as well as the negatives about Christianity, it's no wonder that this imbalance in media reporting negatively influences people. Even some Christians, let alone non-Christians have become disillusioned with The Church. Media persuasion is strong.

Again, in regard to the media exposed scandals, none of us can say we are not disappointed to learn about them; but that should not be a reason for becoming disillusioned with the entire Church or rejecting all of Christianity. These scandals are a small percentage of the Christian population. Nonetheless, because there have been *some* moral failures, many critics lump all Christians together and generally characterize us as a bunch of hypocrites. It's never wise to generalize and certainly not in this situation. Why vilify all of the faithful men and women serving God because of a few weak vessels?

It's All About Money

Why is it that many church ministers, evangelists, and other Christian television and radio broadcasters who ask for financial support, are labeled "charlatans" and "money-grabbers?" Never mind that we know, as the media does, that it takes millions of dollars to broadcast by radio or television and to take the gospel throughout the world as Jesus commissioned them to do. These characterizations are unfair, and give wrong impressions of the good Christians who conduct themselves in an honorable way and in accordance with the standards of the Bible. We are all aware that the news media does little reporting of "good news." Unfortunately, non-Christians, especially, have no way of knowing the millions of exemplary Christian leaders among us, who are faithful to God, His calling to serve Him, and are faithful in how they spend His money. There are honorable men and women in Christian leadership who are faithfully serving God diligently and tirelessly. Some of them preach from pulpits or publish the good news of the gospel and others broadcast it by Christian television and radio. Because of these honorable and dedicated servants of God, multiplied millions of unbelievers throughout the world have become born again into a *new life,* and multiplied millions of Christians are continually edified in their faith—and remember, it all costs multiplied millions of dollars.

Mega Church Mania

There is another source of negative influence that, sadly, causes some of us to be skeptical and others to get all worked up and become critical and judgmental. It's the "Mega Churches!" Some Christians, who prefer a traditional, quiet and structured church service, think them loud, and rather extreme, with their blaring musical instruments and overly emotional worship and criticize them for it. They judge them to be too lively and even irreverent. The problem is, many of these Christians have never stepped foot inside of one of these *Mega Churches* but have only heard about them or had a momentary look at their services on TV. Unknowingly, they are forgetting that the Scriptures tell us these services perfectly fit God's biblical description for worship services: "Shout joyfully to the Lord, all the earth: make a loud noise, and rejoice, and sing praises... Praise the Lord! Praise God in His sanctuary: praise Him in the firmament of His power. Praise Him for His mighty acts: praise Him according to His excellent greatness. Praise Him with the sound of the trumpet: praise Him with the harp. Praise Him with the timbrel and dance: praise Him with stringed instruments and organs. Praise Him upon the loud cymbals: praise Him upon the high sounding cymbals. Let every thing that hath breath praise the Lord. Praise ye the Lord" (Ps. 98:4 and Ps.150.) Perhaps it's time we prayerfully consider adjusting our thinking to align with God's thinking in His Word.

Also, the media obviously has an interest in these non-denominational *Mega Churches* that adhere only to the Bible, especially those that are fast growing; with congregations made up of some of the born again believers who were once members of one of the mainline denominational churches. They target them for scrutiny, along with the evangelistic, stadium-sized gatherings, like those in which Billy Graham once preached, and others preach today. Then, there are television investigative news programs, which have done exposés from time to time on a *Mega Church* or an evangelistic ministry and portrayed them and their clergy and leaders in a negative light. Has the media ever uncovered a ministry that is actually unethical in its leadership and operations according to Bible standards? Unfortunately, that answer is, "Yes." Just as there have been some exposed secular corporations, which had CEO's or board trustees who operated them in an unethical manner. It happens everywhere. But when it comes to Christian ministries, it's a small percentage; and I believe that if a particular one is not of God, it will not last, anyway. However, it may do some damage before it drops out of sight, which is disturbing to all true followers of Christ.

On the other hand, I personally know church and evangelistic ministries, which are totally aligned with the Bible's standard. Nevertheless, TV national network investigative programs have targeted them for exposés, because of "alleged" charges, which are broadcast around the world. After the fact, every suspected detail that can be dug up on its leadership or operation is dissected and scrutinized. Although a thorough investigation finds no fault and the ministry proves to have sterling leadership and operation, the television exposure of *alleged* charges alone is powerful enough to have fueled the fire of suspicion about its validity — and can cause people to turn away from good ministry.

I believe any true ministry of God can stand rigorous investigation in every area of its leadership and operation. And many have. Let's look at a comparative story in Scripture that tells about the same type *alleged* or trumped up charges, false accusations, criticisms, presumptions and judgments made against the first Church of Jesus Christ and its 12 Disciples *(the preachers and evangelists of that day)*. In Acts 5, we are told that the religious leaders of the Sanhedrin, made charges against the apostles, when they brought them before the Council: The Bible states, "They were furious *(meaning the religious leaders)* and plotted to kill them. Then one very wise man in the council stood up. He was a Pharisee named Gamaliel, a teacher of the law held in respect by all the people. He commanded the Council to put the apostles outside for a while. Then he said to them: "Men of Israel... keep away from these men and let them alone; for if this plan or this work is of men, it will come to nothing; but if it is of God, you cannot overthrow it—lest you even be found to fight against God" (See Acts 5:33-39, NKJV, Italics added).

Something for all of us to ponder and pray about.

Christianity in America Is Failing

Now, let's look at the negative perception of "separation of church and state." For one thing, this phrase is not even included in our *Constitution* but it surely causes a great deal of confusion. My opinion on this is purely subjective, but I believe that while efforts for s*eparation of church and state* have had some measures of success, they will never fully succeed because: Despite efforts to stop prayer in public schools; to stop military Chaplains from praying in the Name of Jesus; to remove symbols of our Judeo-Christian heritage from our national landscape; to relentlessly mock Christians on television and in movies and entertainment; to publicize the moral failures of only some Christians; to emphasize the fact that some Christians have left their churches for various reasons; and despite the fact that there is ongoing confusion and controversy among we *imperfect* Christians and divisions among our *imperfect* churches, God still lives in the individual hearts of His people. Believers still pray. Both their prayers and the symbols of their faith will always live in their hearts. Prayer is still the most powerful thing on earth and God still honors the prayers of His people, according to His Will. The Bible still holds the answers to the world, national, and personal problems of mankind. The Holy Spirit still moves to perform the Word of God. There are still Bible-believing, God-anointed clergy and teachers to advance the truth of the Bible, and the Gospel of Jesus Christ; which still brings new converts into the faith. And God still protects, and pours out blessings, and does miracles for His people.

Church and State will never be separated for people of God. We know that our nation's justice system and the laws of our land were founded on the laws of God, according to the Bible. Our Judeo-Christian heritage will never be eradicated from the consciousness of our nation's true believers. Jesus made this statement about "The Church": "The gates of hell shall not prevail against it" (Matt. 16:18b). Notice that He did not declare that there would not be some individuals and entities that would come against *The Church,* only that no efforts in doing so will prevail! Because of our perfect, loving, forgiving, restoring Jesus Christ and because of His sacrifice on the cross and His resurrection—*The Church* and Christianity is not only very much alive today, but also, it keeps growing in America. Something else for us to ponder and pray about.

Christianity Worldwide Is Failing

When it comes to Christianity in this day and age, we also hear and see media reports that Christians are leaving churches in droves. Naturally, some people do leave their churches. Christians have left Protestant denominations and the Catholic Church as well, for a variety of reasons. Perhaps many of those "leaving" churches are simply moving from one church to another, to find the church that fits their comfort level. These are some of the people who created the *Mega Churches* and continue to add to their phenomenal growth. After all, we believers are a diverse group of people and we have diverse ways of expressing our Christian faith. The publication, *Christianity Today—General Statistics and Facts of Christianity,* which offers the most current facts available, prove the true state of Christianity in the world today. It states that Christianity is ranked as the largest religion in the world today, with 2.18 billion adherents.

Media reports would make us think most of the U.S. and world population no longer believes Christian principles are beneficial to live by or for solving world, national and personal problems; and that people have given up on finding hope and help in Jesus Christ and The Church. To me, this statistic does not sound like our Christian Churches worldwide are failing at all. Again, something more for all of us to ponder and pray about.

At this point, we have covered Scripture, subjective commentary, and recorded facts and statistics. Hopefully, we have shed new light on some of the *misconceptions* and *negative perceptions* about Christians, The Church, and Christianity as a whole, which can help those who have been skeptical to be more receptive to *the promise of new life*. It may be clear by now whether or not being born again of the Spirit *is* for you. If it is, congratulations, you have made the best decision of your life. However, if you still are undecided, perhaps the upcoming last chapter will give you even more understanding of what to expect when you do decide to make the choice that will transform your life.

Chapter Fourteen

NEW LIFE, BORN AGAIN...
WHAT DO YOU WANT?

T his final chapter gives us the opportunity to share more personally *woman-to-woman, heart-to-heart.* Psalm 139 tells us that
our All-Knowing God knew us from the womb: "You made all the
delicate, inner parts of my body and knit me together in my mother's womb. You watched me as I was being formed in utter seclu-
sion...You saw me before I was born. Every day of my life was
recorded in your book. Every moment was laid out before a single
day had passed. How precious are your thoughts about me, O God!"
(Psalm 139:13-17, NLT).

How *precious,* indeed, is that Scripture. In fact, many years
ago I first read that Scripture in the King James Bible and I took
courage from the Psalmist David's words: "In Your book my days
were written and fashioned, when as yet there was none of them *(or
before I began to live them)"* (Verse16, Italics added). I was convinced beyond a shadow of doubt then as I am now, to believe that
from the womb God knew the end from the beginning of my life.
And I believe it's true of your life, too.

Another Scripture we can all take courage from declares: "For
I know the thoughts and plans that I have for you, says the Lord,
thoughts and plans for welfare and peace and not for evil, to give
you hope in your final outcome. Then you will call upon Me, inquire

for, and require Me as a vital necessity and find Me, when you search for Me with all your heart." (See Jer. 29:11-13. AMP.) I believe that applies to you, me, and every other person God has created.

The thought occurs to me again that some of us might forget that even before we call on God, He knows each of us—even though we don't know Him as yet. God is constantly seeing and hearing our heart, like He saw and heard the heart of Cornelius, the Italian Gentile and Roman Centurion whose story you read in Chapter Five. And I have learned that God is working behind the scenes in our lives, even though we might be yet unaware. God is ever patient, and ready to bring about His special intentions—His *'thoughts and plans'* for us. But, we have to do our part by *searching for Him with all of our heart.* As written in several ways throughout these chapters, the Lord is waiting to meet each of us right where we are, according to what He already knows about us—and our hearts.

I trust that most of you knew exactly where you were spiritually when you began reading *The Promise of New Life*. And, hopefully, through its biblical and present-day content you have gained knowledge and understanding of what this *new life* in Christ means and how to experience being born again of the Spirit and, thereby, *empowered*. Now, having had the opportunity throughout the previous chapters to examine where you are spiritually, according to Scripture, and where you want to be, I wish to ask you the same question this chapter title asks: *New Life, Born Again… What Do You Want?*

If, at this point, you know you are still not ready to make your decision to be born again, that's okay. No pressure. With Jesus, there is never pressure. Whatever the reason you are not ready is between you and God. He has given each of us our own free will to decide whether or not we want to make our commitment to follow Christ— and exactly when. I've learned that God's timing is always perfect. God doesn't want robot-like followers. He wants us to choose by our own free will to follow Christ and to know why we love and trust in Him and His Word. While the choice is, indeed, yours, I want to make sure you don't hold back for the wrong reasons. Let's get even more personal *woman-to-woman, heart-to-heart* in these last pages.

I encourage you to remember that no matter what your life condition is, you were not an accident. God made "you" on purpose, exactly as you are; and He wants to fellowship with "you"—no matter how many other sons and daughters He has. Also I can assure you that God has good intentions for you. The Word says it is already in the mind of God what are the *'thoughts and plans'* hidden in His heart and already *written in His book* for you. He has *'thoughts and plans'* about which you will only know when you exercise your faith to become born again of the Spirit. The Bible declares: "Now faith is the substance of things hoped for, the evidence of things not seen" (Heb. 11:1).

Let me assure you that there is nothing you have ever done since God saw you in your mother's womb that would keep Him from lovingly giving you *new life* in Christ. Contrary to what you think about yourself or what other people might think about you—on the authority of God's Word I guarantee that you or no other human being is too sinful nor is your life condition and circumstances so extreme, so dark or so tragic that Jesus Christ will not forgive, save and transform you. The Bible makes clear that we are all the same:

- "We like sheep have gone astray; we have turned every one to his own way; and the Lord hath laid on him *(Jesus)* the inequity of us all" (Isa. 53:6, Italics added).
- "There is no one righteous, not even one... there is no one who does good, not even one" (See Rom. 3:10-12b).
- "If we say that we have no sin, we deceive ourselves, and the truth is not in us" (I John 1:8).
- "If we say that we have not sinned, we make Him *(God)* a liar, and His Word is not in us" (I John 1:10, Italics added).
- "If we confess our sins, He is faithful and just to forgive us our sins, and to cleanse us from all unrighteousness" (I John 1:9).

God requires honesty. Jesus came to earth and died to pay *your* sin debt. He would have suffered, shed His blood and died just for *you*. His free gift of salvation and His power can liberate *you* from *your* sin life, and His Bible truth can overcome any negative, self-condemning, self-defeating thoughts you have about yourself. Even when we see the truth about ourselves, still we can't get good enough to gain *new life* in Christ by trying to "clean up our act" before we come to Jesus. No point. Because we actually need Him in order to do that. Jesus called each biblical character and each contemporary woman you've read about here, to come to Him just as they were. Jesus is the One who *cleaned up their act* and transformed them. So, I encourage you to believe that there is nothing you need to do but accept the free gift God has for you.

If you still haven't made your decision to be born again, but what you've read thus far is resonating in your *heart* and *spirit*; then, you might consider that it may be the Spirit of God "prompting" you. God encourages all of us in His Word, "Today, if you would hear His voice and when you hear it, do not harden your hearts" (Heb. 4:7b, AMP). I implore you, please don't ignore this *prompting* or this voice of the Spirit, and don't be afraid of it. God is presenting you with the opportunity to choose His *promise of new life*.

But making your decision could, indeed, be more difficult if you are one who needs to intellectually understand every detail of this spiritual *new life* before you choose to experience it. Be certain that doesn't bother God by any means. God is the ultimate intellectual — He is All-Knowing. If an intellectual is sincerely searching to know if there is a God, Who He is, and how to connect with Him, he or she gets God's attention the same as anyone else. Although it is only by faith you can receive God's first promise to become born again; the Bible also makes clear that God gave you your intellect. So, obviously, He doesn't mind if in your search for spiritual truth, that you use it to question and analyze what you have heard in the past, what you are reading here, and what the Bible says.

Remember some of the biblical characters whose stories you read in Chapter Five were intellectual, educated and prominent. For example, you read that Nicodemus was learned in the Old Testament Scriptures and an important leader in the Synagogue. Saul of Tarsus was from an aristocratic family and had been educated in the Old Testament Law by Gamaliel, who was a leading scholar and teacher in the Synagogue; and after Saul's conversion, he became the "Apostle Paul" and writer of two-thirds of the New Testament. Cornelius was a Roman Centurion, who had 100 men under his command. And let me add, Luke. You will recall that Luke was neither a Jew nor one of Jesus' 12 disciples, but he was a Gentile; educated, a medical physician by profession, a companion to the Apostle Paul, and he also wrote the Gospel of Luke and The Book of Acts in the New Testament.

I can assure you that over the years of my public ministry, I have personally known members of the Catholic, Protestant, and Jewish faiths, who were quite intellectual. Like Nicodemos, they practiced the sacraments and traditions of their particular religions, yet, were still seeking *something more* to help them feel connected to God. Being truly connected to the Living God is not about "religion." It is about "relationship." He saw their individual hearts and began leading each one in a unique way. Some were well educated, successful, and socially prominent; in fact, a few were wealthy men and women who were, nonetheless, intellectual seekers of spiritual truth. And some of those who were not churchgoers, were not opposed to Jesus Christ or Christianity but after hearing Bible truth, they just needed to take the time to intellectually understand more about the born again experience. I know each of their stories and how God worked in their lives. In their search, some of them studied various "philosophies of men." However, the Bible declares: "Beware lest anyone cheat you through philosophy and empty deceit, according to the tradition of men, according to the basic principles of the world, and not according to Christ" (Col. 2:8, NKJV). Suffice it to say, I also know that they neither found God in those *philosophies of men* nor did they find a permanent peace, transformation or satisfaction for a better life. So they kept searching.

When each of these intellectual seekers of truth found Jesus Christ, their search was over. Why? Because there was a moment in time when they heard or read Bible truth about how to know God by becoming born again. With faith, they opened their *heart* to this truth and Jesus revealed Himself to them in a way that was uniquely designed just for them. How did something that mysterious, that miraculous happen to them? It was simply Bible truth, the words of Jesus Christ, Himself: "You must be born again" that they chose to believe with their heart—and they were saved. In other words, at their personal *moment in time,* they exercised their faith and had a "heart experience" with Christ, which by-passed all their intellectualizing and analyzing efforts. Jesus did for them what the Bible promises: "If

179

you confess with your mouth that Jesus is Lord and believe in your heart that God raised him from the dead, you will be saved. For it is by believing in your heart that you are made right with God, and it is by confessing with your mouth that you are saved" (Rom. 10:9-10).

Yes, with their heart they believed and made their confession of faith. Jesus forgave and cleansed them from all their sin and guilt; He took up residence in their heart; and He brought His love, peace, and joy into their *new life*. Thus, the Word of God proved true to them, experientially, and they knew for the first time that they had become connected to the Living God. The Bible promises: "When they call on Me, I will answer; I will be with them in trouble. I will rescue them and honor them. I will reward them with a long life" (Psalm 91:15-16, NLT).

God's *sovereignty* remains, when it comes to His unique ways of revealing Himself to humanity. As we saw in the stories earlier, some experiences are dramatic and others are simple. There are many variations and sovereign administrations of God, which the Holy Spirit uses to draw believers to a *new life* in Christ. However, each individual receives Jesus Christ by faith, only. It's personal.

I always think it is fascinating when we can read or hear a testimony about receiving Christ and becoming born again, from a person clear across the world, who lives in an entirely different culture and speaks a different language. We will find him using the same phrases to describe his born again experience. Find a translator and we will hear that he, just as believers in any other part of the world, is expressing the same results: "I felt like a new person... I knew my sins were forgiven... I felt clean inside... I felt a new love... new peace... new joy... after Jesus Christ came into my heart."

When millions of people, both intelligent and unlearned, from every culture on earth begin their own search for God in their own way and encounter Christ in a way only God can orchestrate and they come to the same truth as all the others—it seems to me that is much more than coincidence and should be seriously considered.

While reading this book, you have been up close and personal with the Living God through His Bible truth and the testimonies of His people. He is, indeed, a great God, Who proves Himself when challenged and shares Himself when invited in. If you will challenge Him, He will prove Himself to you. If you will invite Him in, He will do for you what He has done for me and the others whose stories you have read.

If you do make your decision to choose *the promise of new life,* I think you will consider it to be the most important decision you will make in your lifetime. At the moment it happens, you will know your sin-slate of the past has been wiped clean. You will have been given a second chance to live your life with God's love and to make up for your past mistakes with others. Forgiveness for your sins of the past will change everything. God promises He will not remember your sins. Your past will be just that — your *past.* You will no longer need to appear to be what others have *labeled* you. You will be free from other people's expectations for you, too. Remember, God does not define you by your past. He only sees you as the woman He created you to be. You will know what every other born again believer knows: that your *spirit has come alive;* that you are connected to the Triune God — God the Father, God the Son, and God the Holy Spirit; and that you have perfect assurance of your eternal life. God will confirm to you by His Spirit within that you have the *real deal.* You will desire to read the Bible — and you *will* understand it.

You will know you have had a "mountaintop" experience. However, there *will* come "valleys." The Bible does not guarantee you a smooth, untroubled, crisis-free life because you're born again. Although you now have that solid Bible foundation, it will not insulate you against the storms of life. We live in a fallen world and, therefore, we never know what another day will bring. Jesus promises that in your trials He will be with you. The Holy Spirit will give you God's wisdom and counsel, if you ask for it. Your trust and confidence will be in the faithfulness of Jesus to help you to not only "survive" your trials but also, to "thrive" in the midst of them — *thrive* until He either delivers you completely out of your trial or "sustains" you while you go through to the other side of it. Either way you will know victory. Therefore, with your faith and trust in God, the storms of life will never overwhelm you. For born again believers, the Bible declares: "We are troubled on every side, yet not distressed; we are perplexed, but not in despair; persecuted, but not forsaken; cast down, but not destroyed" (II Cor. 4:8-9).

Jesus will be living in your *heart* and will finally have His *rightful place* for you to know His constant companionship—and His purpose. You will be *empowered* to live your Christian life. Your unwavering faith in God's Word will cause the power of the Holy Spirit to bless your life and give honor and glory to Jesus Christ: "Now to Him who is able to do exceedingly abundantly above all that we ask or think, according to the power that works in us" (Eph. 3:20).

It has been learned and, in fact, proven in the lives of this author and the women you've met herein as well as great numbers of other believers I know personally, that when you are born again, you will not only receive God's enabling power to deal with all of your challenges and trials but also, to fulfill His plan for your life. God will use your talents and abilities and, moreover, He will surprise you by releasing new abilities through you to equip and enable you to do what you never dreamed you were capable of doing: "Eye has not seen nor ear heard, nor have entered into the heart of man, the things which God has prepared for them that love Him" (I Cor. 2:9).

You will live the rest of your life knowing that God loves you unconditionally. And not only will you live with God's love for you and with your true love *for* God and others but also, you will have a healthy love for yourself. You will desire to "look your best, do your best, and be your best," which the Bible will help you achieve, to feel good about yourself and feel good about the *'happy, self-confident, unflappable'* image you project everywhere you go as an *empowered Christian woman*. On the authority of the Bible, I guarantee that you will enjoy living your new *empowered* life. Without hesitation, I promise that you will like the woman you become. The choice is yours.

I leave you with these last words:

It has been my joy, pleasure, and privilege to have this time of sharing with you, *woman-to-woman, heart-to-heart*. When the Lord first impressed me to write this book, I am convinced that God already knew how He intended to bless you with its message. I trust you gained more spiritual knowledge and were persuaded of God's unconditional love for you through its Bible truth. I thank you for graciously reading my heart-driven words as well as those of the six other women, who so aptly and sincerely shared their testimonies with you. We each pray our stories inspired and encouraged you.

While our time together in this book has ended, I encourage you to keep moving forward on your spiritual journey; and I invite you to join me in exploring more Bible truth in my second book, *The Empowered Christian Woman: The Promise of Power.* In it, we will discover together who the "Person" of God the Holy Spirit is, what His functions are and how He intends to use them to guide each of our lives. Again, you will see the evidence of this truth revealed in the featured stories of the same contemporary women you have come to know.

I pray you will be as hopeful and uplifted as I am, by this divinely inspired scriptural promise God makes to all of humanity: "The Lord earnestly waits, expecting, looking, and longing to be gracious to you; and therefore He lifts Himself up, that He may have mercy on you and show loving-kindness to you. For the Lord is a God of justice. Blessed, happy, fortunate, to be envied are all those who earnestly wait for Him, who expect and look and long for Him [for His victory, His favor, His love, His peace, His joy, and His matchless, unbroken companionship!]" (Isaiah 30:18, AMP).

The End

THE CHRISTIAN CONFESSION AND PRAYER TO RECEIVE THE PROMISE OF NEW LIFE

Y ou will probably want to use your own words to speak to God. The following is offered simply as a supporting sample:

Father God, I believe the Bible truth I have read about You in this book. I now believe that there is only one way to receive the "promise of new life" to become born again and connected with You, and that is through faith in Your Only Begotten Son, Jesus Christ. I believe You sent Jesus to earth and He lived a sinless life; that He willingly shed His blood and died on the cross for my sins; and I believe Jesus was buried and after three days He arose from the tomb. With His purpose here on earth finished, I believe Jesus ascended back to heaven; and He sent the Holy Spirit to be my Guide in all things. And I believe Jesus is coming again. Now, I also understand that Jesus is my only Mediator between You, Father God, and me; and I believe You love me unconditionally and You have a good plan for my life.

Dear Jesus, I confess to you that I am a sinner in need of Your forgiveness and ask You to come into my heart to live forever. Thank You for Your mercy and assurance of my eternal home in heaven. And thank You for giving me the "promise of new life" to be born again to live the abundant life You came to give me to live as an "empowered Christian woman." From this day forward, I commit myself to follow You; and as the Holy Spirit leads, I will witness to others about Christ's great love for them.

In Your Name I pray. Amen

WOMEN WHO CONTRIBUTED THEIR STORIES

Joy Briggs (Mrs. William)
Greensboro, N. C.
bill.briggs51@gmail.com

Elaine Keith (Mrs. Bill)
Columbus, Ohio
EM: cflslc@sbglobal.net

Cara Suchman (Mrs. Edward)
Mt. Vernon, Ohio
EM: carasuchman@gmail.com

Ruth Foster (Mrs. Ralph)
Columbus, Ohio
EM: pharmosu1956@gmail.com

Joyce Marion (Mrs. Berkly)
Lancaster, Ohio
EM: bmarion@columbus.rr.com

Judy Ross (Mrs. Mike)
Milton, West Virginia
EM: mikejudy247@gmail.com

Anita Lantz (Author)
Columbus, Ohio
EM: alantz1215@gmail.com

CPSIA information can be obtained
at www.ICGtesting.com
Printed in the USA
FFOW02n0923291216
30701FF